Applied Strategic Management

OrangeBooks Publication

Smriti Nagar, Bhilai, Chhattisgarh - 490020

Website:**www.orangebooks.in**

© **Copyright, 2022, Author**

All rights reserved. No part of this book may be reproduced, stored in a retrieval system, or transmitted, in any form by any means, electronic, mechanical, magnetic, optical, chemical, manual, photocopying, recording or otherwise, without the prior written consent of its writer.

APPLIED STRATEGIC MANAGEMENT

Distinctive Positioning is the Key to Success

Dr. Sanjay Saxena

OrangeBooks Publication
www.orangebooks.in

INDEX

Chapter 1
Strategic Positioning 1
    1.1 Why Strategy? 1
    1.2 Distinctive Strategic Positioning 2
    1.3 Strategic Fit 7
    1.4 The Sources of Strategic Positions 9
    1.5 Strategic Management Model 14

Chapter 2
Strategic Analysis 16
    2.1 Types of Strategic Analysis 16
    2.2 PESTLE Analysis 18
    2.3 Five Forces Analysis 26
    2.4 BCG Matrix 37
    2.5 SWOT Analysis 41
    2.6 Value Chain Analysis 46
    2.7 Resource-Based View (RBV) 52

Chapter 3
Strategic Choices (Corporate Level) 58
    3.1 Strategies at Different Levels 58
    3.2 Corporate-Level Strategies 60
    3.3 Stability Strategies 60
    3.4 Growth Strategies 62
    3.5 Integration Strategies 72
    3.6 Retrenchment Strategies 82

Chapter 4
Strategic Choices (Business-Level).. 95
4.1 Business-Level Strategies.. 95
4.2 Porter's Generic Strategies... 97
4.3 Blue Ocean Strategy 110
4.4 Disruptive Strategy 130
4.5 Jobs-To-Be-Done Strategy 136

Chapter 5
Strategic Implementation.. 142
5.1 Activities Under Strategic Implementation 142
5.2 Resource Allocation 142
5.3 Restructuring Organizational Structure 143
5.4 Business Process Reengineering 145
5.5 Staffing 149
5.6 Building Leadership at All Levels... 156
5.7 Functions of Leadership 159

Chapter 6
Measuring Outcomes 194
6.1 Measuring Firm's Performance 194
6.2 HR Outcomes 196
6.3 Organizational Outcomes 199
6.4 Financial Outcomes 200
6.5 Customer Outcomes 202

References..205

Chapter 1

Strategic Positioning

1.1 Why Strategy?

Today, in the digital era, most business enterprises struggle to compete in the market for three core reasons. Firstly, due to multi-brand online stores such as Amazon and Flipkart, the customers' access, and sales & distribution barriers are completely shredded, and any enterprise can upload and sell its products across the globe. Secondly, customers have complete information regarding various companies, products, brands, quality standards, price ranges, and customer reviews, therefore, it has become exceedingly challenging for any company to establish itself in the market and profitably sell its products. Thirdly due to the above-mentioned scenario, most business enterprises are striving hard to become the best and leave competitors behind in terms of price, product quality, and before or after-sales services. To be the best (in price, quality, and service), adapt quickly to a fast-changing market, and sustain in the market, enterprises need to keep their operational efficiency much better than the competitors, which is not possible for most of them.

Almost all the top companies are consistently benchmarking to achieve best practices and develop specific core competencies to keep themselves ahead of competitors. They are adopting various management tools and techniques such as total quality management, outsourcing, benchmarking, partnering, business process reengineering, restructuring, and change management to improve productivity and quality. Still, they cannot sustain a competitive advantage because their competitors are also adopting the same techniques and generating the same level of productivity, quality, and efficiency.

Competing based on operational efficiencies raises the bar of productivity and quality, but in this process, all the companies start looking alike regarding price, product quality, and services. Ultimately all companies reach a level from where further improvement in operational efficiencies at a specific price becomes impossible. In this situation, companies have limited options such as acquisition or merger to survive in the competitive environment. Therefore, operational efficiency is necessary but not enough. Companies are failing to create their distinct position in the market and look unique to consumers. To outperform the competitors, we need to differentiate ourselves from rivals in terms of providing unique value to customers.

1.2 Distinctive Strategic Positioning

Distinctive strategic positioning is the enterprise's business strategy to uniquely position itself in the market and compete with rivals by performing similar activities differently or performing entirely different activities. Therefore, strategy is all about becoming unique and not the best. The strategy is a plan of action to create a unique position in the market and deliver unique value to the customers, and in turn, provide a competitive advantage to the enterprise over rivals. Different strategic positions must have different sets of activities. With the same set of activities, an enterprise cannot establish a distinctive strategic position in the market and cannot achieve a sustained competitive advantage against rivals. An enterprise may not distinctively position itself in the market unless it embraces some trade-offs associated with its unique business strategies.

Uniqueness Require Trade-offs

Trade-offs occur when activities under two different strategies are incompatible with each other. For example, Continental Lite Airlines paid a heavy penalty while trying to be a low-cost airline on some routes and a full-service airline on different routes. It failed to incorporate and link all the activities that can adequately reduce the cost to offer low fares to passengers. As a result, to offer low fares on some routes, it had to dilute its profits generated from full-service routes.

Reckitt Benckiser's Dettol medicated soap, Dettol liquid handwash, Dettol hand sanitizer, and Dettol antiseptic liquid are well-established brands in India, and customers prefer to buy these products regularly. But when Reckitt and Benckiser launched a beauty soap having high moisturizer and good fragrance with the brand name Dettol, it failed in the market. We must choose what not to do while developing a distinctive strategy to compete in the market. For example, medical soap manufacturing companies sacrifice the deodorant market, unbelievably expensive luxury car-making companies avoid making low-cost cars, or premium airlines avoid starting low-cost services. In addition, it isn't easy to keep two or three contrasting target segments within the same product line because there is every possibility that you may lose all the segments. For example, Volkswagen has always been in-demand for making affordable cars catering to the masses. So, when Volkswagen announced a luxury car called Phaeton, its regular buyers couldn't afford to buy this car and shifted to other affordable brands. At the same time, the premium buyers didn't accept the

Phaeton brand, because Volkswagen is known for making affordable cars for the masses.

Trade-offs arise basically for three reasons, which are narrated hereunder:

1. **Image of the Company:** Mercedes Benz has an image and reputation for manufacturing high-quality luxurious cars for a rich class of people, but if they start making low-cost cars for middle-class people, their image of making premium cars will be tarnished, and they will lose their premium segment.
2. **Different Sets of Activities:** Different strategic positions require a different set of product design, raw materials, equipment, employees' skills, and management systems. For example, suppose a full-service airline wants to start low service airline, it requires aircraft with no business class, low running cost, less expensive secondary airports, fast turnaround time, no check-in baggage facility, no boarding pass, no allotment of seat numbers, massive reduction in the number of employees, elimination of hierarchical organizational structure, and employees with multiple skills and so on.
3. **Organizational Priorities:** In many organizations, the senior management makes organizational priorities very clear such as producing high-quality, luxurious products or low-cost products, serving premium segment or low-price segments, serving institutions and industries, serving retail customers, and so on. Based on these priorities, enterprises need to choose what not to do.

False Trade-offs Between Cost and Quality

Most companies try to position themselves in the market by providing better quality at a lower cost without realizing that already they are incurring unnecessary costs such as redundant processes, wasted efforts, poor control or accuracy, and weak coordination. Reducing these unnecessarily inflated costs will not provide a sustained competitive advantage as there is no real cost reduction. For example, many manufacturing units operate with many defects in the products due to poor quality control throughout the process workflow. They are also operating at an excessive cost due to overproduction, excess downtime or changeover time, excess inventory, excess transportation cost within the factory because of poor layout, excess processing (redundant processes), and excess motion of raw materials, people, and equipment. Reducing costs on these fronts is not a real cost reduction. Instead, it is a reduction in inflated costs. Any effort to adopt a low-cost strategy by reducing inflated costs is destined to fail in the market. Therefore, to take distinctive positioning with a low-cost strategy, enterprises must identify and reduce the real costs.

Why Enterprises Are Failing to Create Distinctive Positions?

Companies fail to choose a distinctive position in the market for a variety of reasons. One of the most common reasons is a 'desire to grow.' The managers are under constant pressure to grow fast, even if they need to avoid their company's distinctive position. Eventually, managers dilute the company's distinctive position by increasing the existing product lines; adding new product lines; unnecessarily adding too many features to a product; adopting all kinds of technologies, services, and processes; and in extreme cases, moving for acquisitions. In their pursuit of growth, managers make compromises and become inconsistent with the company's distinctive strategic position.

In the opposite situation, where all the rivals are operating at a far lower level of productivity, it is easier for a well-run company to beat its ineffective rivals on all fronts at once by just maintaining its operational efficiency. In this situation, taking any distinctive strategic position or embracing trade-offs looks irrelevant. On the contrary, managers consider trade-offs as their weaknesses. But if strong rivals are performing at top levels of operational efficiency, then embracing trade-offs and taking a distinctive strategic position is extremely important to get sustained competitive advantage over them.

Some managers have over infatuation with participating in the technological revolution, and as a result, they want to adopt and use every technology. For this purpose, they go for taking many strategic positions at a time to use various technologies.

In most cases, senior managers fail to focus on creating a specific strategic position in the market because they mainly concentrate on various practices such as benchmarking TQM, Reengineering, and Restructuring, which can enhance operational efficiencies. They get caught up in the trap of operational efficiencies or the competitors' best practices so much that they do not understand the need to develop a strategy. Also, the results of various operational efficiency enhancement programs are very tangible and measurable, and managers can easily project their performance as a great performance in a short period. They get rewards and promotions easily.

Overly customer focus managers think that the company must serve all the customers' needs and demands. This notion of serving all kinds of needs and demands of customers is the major constraint for taking any distinctive strategic position in the market.

1.3 Strategic Fit

Mere taking a distinctive strategic position in the market will not provide any competitive advantage to a company. Distinctive positioning needs the interlocking of various unique decisions and activities within the company. The strategic fit is a fit between chosen strategy and unique activities. The strategy rests on creating a "fit" between strategy and unique activities and interlocking various unique activities within the company. For example, when some airlines tried to copy low-cost point-to-point services Southwest Airlines without developing the whole interlocked system of unique activities, the results were disastrous for them.

Strategic 'Fit' Case of Southwest Airlines

One of the most successful airlines in the USA, Southwest Airlines, adopted a low-cost no-frills strategic position by offering point-to-point convenient flight services at a very low price to daily commuters. To tailor all its activities to deliver low-price convenient service to its passengers, Southwest Airlines focused on point-to-point flight services between midsize and large cities. It utilizes secondary airports in large cities and avoids primary airports to prevent higher airport charges, flight delays, passenger waiting time, and long queues just before runways. It does not fly great distances and maintains fast 15 minutes turnaround time so that the aircraft are quickly ready to fly again. It helps airlines to utilize their aircraft to operate more flights in a day. operate more flights with fewer aircraft. To reduce the aircraft's maintenance cost and increase efficiency, it keeps a fleet of only one aircraft type, i.e., boing 737 aircraft. Having only one type of aircraft reduces the inventory of spare parts and employee training costs and increases maintenance efficiencies. Its successful fuel hedging program (long-term contract with oil companies to buy fuel) has reduced a major fraction of its operating expense, which is around 25% cheaper than its competitors. It keeps fewer highly motivated employees and pilots who are not members of the union and can fly long hours to reduce operational costs. On average, they use 94 employees per Southwest aircraft in contrast to competitors who use 130. One Southwest staff serves on average 2500 passengers per year compared to competitors' staff serving 1000 passengers per year.

It is now evident that Southwest Airlines got a sustained competitive advantage because of its interlocked activities. All the activities contribute to the company's low-cost strategy and reinforce one another. It is extremely difficult for the rivals to imitate the whole system of interlocked activities. Therefore, strategic 'fit' provides a sustained competitive advantage to the companies. Moreover, distinctive strategic positions developed on the interlocked system of unique activities are more sustainable than the position taken on individual competencies.

1.4 The Sources of Strategic Positions

As shown in figure 1.1, various strategic positions originate from five diverse sources.

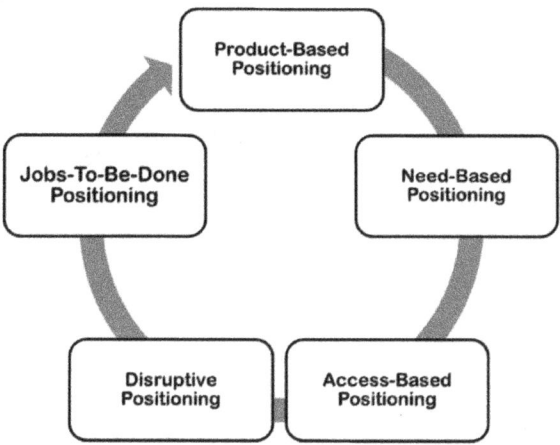

Figure 1.1: Sources of Strategic Positions

1. Product-Based Positioning

Companies try to position themselves in the market based on the range of products or services it offers to customers. Under product-based positioning, companies present the benefits of a variety of products to a particular target audience. For example, In India, many restaurants on the highways, provide a large variety of food to travelers. In addition, large apparel stores such as Pantaloon, Reliance Trends Retail Stores, Globus Fashion Stores, and TATA CLiQ provide a wide range of T-shirts, shirts, trousers, jeans, jackets, designer suits, and shoes to customers. In the healthcare industry, large multispecialty hospitals provide a range of medical treatments in the field of neurology, gynecology, endocrinology, orthopedics, cardiology, and general medicine. These hospitals position themselves based on a range of medical services under one roof. Various OTT platforms such as Netflix and Amazon Prime are competing based on a large variety of good quality content ranging from movies, web series, TV shows, and videos in different languages. Snapple Beverage Corp. adopted product-based positioning and positioned its beverages in 58 flavors.

Picture 1.1: Snapple Beverage in Various Flavors

2. **Need-Based Strategic Positioning**

    Need-based positioning arises when you address most or all the needs of a specific customer segment. Circumstances and time of purchase are also particularly important because the same product satisfy different needs at different time. For example, people going to the office in the morning hours buy coffee from coffee shops to get morning energy while commuting to their offices. People drink the same coffee in the evening at the restaurant for getting relaxed. They also go to a coffee shop if they want to meet their clients outside the office premise.

    A distinctive strategic position based on a unique set of needs will not be translated into a meaningful position unless the set of activities to satisfy it are different and unique. Companies may not differentiate themselves if they want to satisfy different needs with the same set of activities. In this case, competitors will imitate easily.

Starbucks Corporation is an American multinational chain of coffeehouses and roastery reserves headquartered in Seattle, Washington. It is the world's largest coffeehouse chain. As of November 2021, the company had 33,833 stores in 80 countries. It started serving coffee as an experience that satisfies the different physical and emotional needs of customers. Starbucks adopted some innovative activities to position itself in the market as a company serving coffee as a wonderful experience of life. They prepare tasty coffee with properly grind coffee seeds and first-time steamed milk and allow customers to sit for long hours with a cup of coffee in the store, which has a beautiful ambiance (beautiful interior and lighting, and soothing music). Starbucks calls its stores the third home for its customers. Store employees are smart and soft-spoken. They call customers by their first names to give them a personal experience.

3. **Access-Based Positioning**

Many companies position themselves in the market based on how they reach their customers or how customers will reach them. They find ways to reach customers across geographical boundaries.

For example, Amazon is selling goods to customers across continents through its online stores. Byju's "Think and Learn Private Ltd. India, launched an online learning App for school and college students with the prime aim of overcoming the problem of access to students. Their online model allowed students to join their courses from anywhere in the world. The University of Phoenix, Arizona, United States offers online degrees & courses to more than 175000 students from across 115 countries. One can easily imagine the geographical reach and scale of the university of phoenix. Various OTT (over-the-top) platforms such as Netflix, Amazon Prime Video, and Zee5 are providing television and film content over the internet at the request of the individual consumer. Netflix has over 182 million subscribers from all over the world. Other than these examples, food delivery companies such as Swiggy and Zomato in India have adopted access-based positioning by taking online orders and delivering food from different restaurants and cloud kitchens to customers' doorsteps.

4. **Disruptive Positioning**

There are so many good quality and expensive products available in the market, having their consumers and non-consumers. Non-consumers are those who cannot afford these products. Under disruptive positioning, a company attracts non-consumers of the expensive product by introducing little inferior quality inexpensive products. These cheaper and inferior-quality products are unattractive to companies making high-quality, expensive products in the same categories. For example, Apple Inc. is not interested in a poor-quality processor in its products, such as iPhone, iPad, or iMac. But Oppo Electronics Corp. is using an inferior quality processor in its Oppo mobiles for iPhone's non-consumers.

5. **Jobs-To-Be-Done Positioning**

According to Clayton M. Christensen, customers are the wrong unit of analysis. Simply knowing our customers and their opinions will not help us develop products or take a position in the market. In jobs-to-be-done positioning, the companies focus on the jobs that cause people to buy a specific product. Companies are developing products and services around a particular job that they will perform for the customers. Under jobs-to-be-done positioning, companies provide solutions that help consumers to make the progress they are struggling to achieve.

For example, people buy a car to perform some basic but different jobs such as getting ultimate comfort while commuting from one place to another, using the car as an office, using the car as a taxi, or using a good-sized car for a large family. The jobs-to-be-done strategy can help companies develop a car to do a specific job and not develop one size fit for all.

In jobs-to-be-done positioning, companies convert their generic products into potential products through innovation, which provides the appropriate solution to customers' specific problems. In other words, we can say that the potential product performs a specific job for a customer

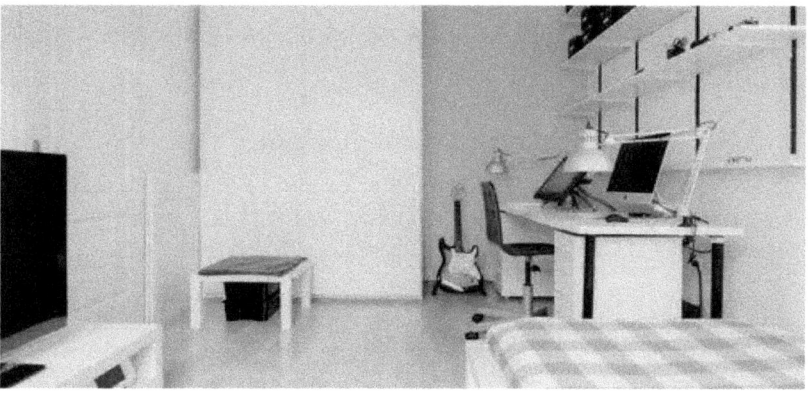

Picture 1.2: Ikea's Jobs-To-Done Positioning

To understand the potential product, let us take an example of the Swedish company Ikea, which manufactures furniture for young professionals living in small homes. They need to furnish their home so that there must be proper utilization of all the corners and empty spaces in the home. Ikea converts its generic furniture into potential furniture by carefully designing furniture so that it should not occupy a large space. At the same time, they should get fit in the corners of the home. Ikea's creative designers are experts in finding and using hidden spaces in small homes. They design furniture so that they occupy little space and can do more than one thing. Ikea takes the challenge to convert a small living room into a room for everyone. They overcome this challenge by developing foldable, flexible, stackable, rollable, and climb-up-on-top-able furniture.

Ikea also takes the challenge of combining two rooms into one with its innovative furnishing, such as combining the bathroom and laundry room into one. Ikea has expertise in providing personal space to people living in shared homes. It can do this even when six persons live together in 40 square meters home. Ikea is the most adorable home furnishing company because they transform each generic product into a potential product, which provides an appropriate solution to certain customers' specific problems.

1.5 Strategic Management Model

Creating distinctive strategic positioning is not just a free choice that a company can make and position itself in the market at once. Distinctive strategic positioning requires an effective plan of action, which can be developed through a continuous and rigorous process of strategic analysis and choosing and implementing the appropriate strategy in the market. We study these processes and sub-processes under strategic management. Therefore, strategic management is a continuous process of various steps such as strategic analysis of the internal and external business environment, making strategic choices, implementing a chosen strategy, and measuring the outcomes. Companies adopt a strategic management process to gain a sustained competitive advantage over competitors.

Figure 1.2: Strategic Management Model

Based on the process definition of strategic management, the four-step strategic management model is used in this book, as shown in figure 1.2.

Chapter 2

Strategic Analysis

2.1 Types of Strategic Analysis

To formulate different competitive strategies, an enterprise needs to make some strategic analysis. It is a process of researching the external and internal business environment in which the firm operates. A business enterprise uses various analytical matrices to do strategic analyses, out of which most business organizations frequently use six important analytical matrices shown in figure 2.1. These analytical matrices are sequentially arranged in an order of analyzing external factors to internal factors.

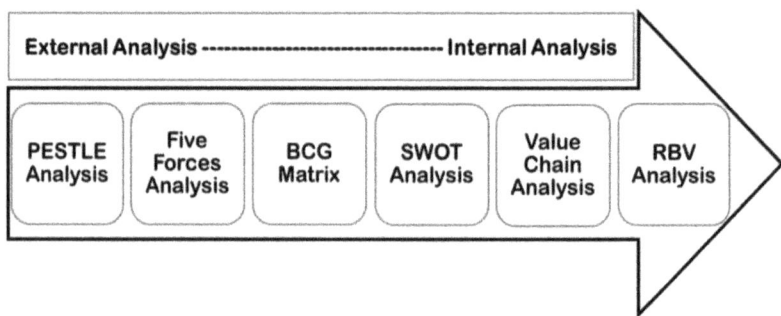

Figure 2.1: Matrices for External and Internal Analyses

The most important matrix used to analyze the external environmental factors is PESTLE Framework. The PESTLE is an acronym for political, economic, social, technological, legal, and environmental factors. This matrix is useful for starting a new business in an existing market, a new market, or a foreign market with an existing business. For taking long-term business decisions, a firm needs to know the stability and current trends of various factors related to the country's PESTLE environments.

Companies are using the **Five Forces Analysis** framework given by Michael Porter to know the attractiveness of an industry for doing business. With this analytical matrix, a firm gets insight into the different forces involved in a particular industry. These five forces are the bargaining power of suppliers, the bargaining power of buyers, the competitive rivalry among the various firms operating within the industry, the threat of substitutes, and the threat of new entrants.

BCG matrix is a framework created by Boston Consulting Group to evaluate the strategic positions of the business portfolios in the light of two parameters. These two parameters are market growth rate and relative market share of different business portfolios. This analysis is done when a firm has various businesses and wants to decide, which business the firm should invest in, and which ones should be divested.

Using **SWOT Analysis**, an enterprise identifies its major strengths and weaknesses, and various opportunities and threats that exist in the market. It helps an enterprise to utilize its strengths in terms of what it does well, overcome its weaknesses, take advantage of existing opportunities, and minimize the risks by avoiding external threats.

Value Chain Analysis is a framework to analyze various internal activities of the enterprise. Its main objective is to recognize, develop, and implement effective processes that may provide a cost advantage over rivals, and create a distinctive strategic position in the market. It also identifies the activities needing improvement in terms of their efficiency and effectiveness.

An enterprise's internal resources are the key to providing a competitive advantage to it. **Resource-Based View (RBV)** is the framework that helps a firm to identify its key resources and improvement required to fulfill the VRIO criteria to provide a competitive advantage to the firm against its rivals. VRIO framework suggests that resources should be Valuable, Rare, Inimitable, and Organizationally Exploitable.

All these analytical matrices mentioned above are being discussed in detail in the coming texts.

2.2 PESTLE Analysis

PESTLE Framework is used to analyze the impact of external environmental factors on business.

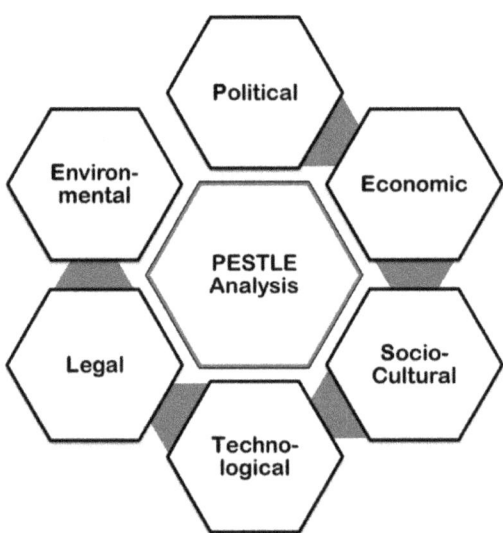

Figure 2.2: PESTLE Framework

As shown in figure 2.2, the PESTLE is an acronym for Political, Economic, Social, Technological, Legal, and Environmental factors that can potentially influence the business and behavior of an enterprise operating in a specific country.

Political Factors

For starting a new business in any country or state, the business firms are primarily interested to know about various political factors such as Govt. stability, bureaucracy, tax policies, corruption level, export or import restrictions, trade union agreements, and property rights.

1. **Govt. Stability**

   If the Govt. is stable, then its various policies would be stable, and as a result, it would be easier for the firms to develop long-term business plans. Moreover, when a political party is making a government with an absolute majority, it is easier for it to draft different bills related to economic and social reforms and get them approved in the country's parliament.

2. **Bureaucracy**

   It is the job of the government to improve the ease of doing business in the country. For example, if the bureaucratic formalities are simple, establishing quickly and running the business smoothly would be quite easier.

3. **Taxation**

   Various taxes on business enterprise affects the cost, which can lead to an increase in the price of the products or services. Indirect taxes also affect businesses in terms of price increases, ease of doing business, and smooth operations. In India, before 2017, there were different tax rates in different states, and due to that, the companies were facing problems in the interstate distribution of goods and services. Dealers were buying goods in the state where the taxes were low and illegally pushing the goods from the backdoor channels to the states where taxes were high. On 1st July 2017, Govt. of India implemented GST (Goods and Services Tax), which replaced all existing multiple taxes imposed by central and state governments. Now business organizations are happy that there is a common tax structure across the country.

4. **Trade Union Agreements**

   Legitimately trade unions are the bodies that protect the rights of the workers so that they get appropriate wages and other benefits and work for legally allowed daily work hours. Trade unions are also responsible for ensuring synergy between employees and employers for the smooth operation of businesses. But due to corruption and personal and political desires, various trade unions misuse their power and get involved in illegal bargains with employers. However, if the trade unions are honest and their agreements are simple and business-friendly, firms may run their businesses smoothly and profitably.

Likewise, there may be various other political factors that can impact the business favorably or adversely. For example, in 2016, Modi Govt. decided to demonetize 1000- and 500-rupee currency notes in India. As a result, industries like real estate, where cash transactions are dominant, got severely affected. Whereas credit and debit card companies and online payment gateways got the benefit of it.

Economic Factors

Economic factors have a direct impact on the growth of businesses in a particular region or country. The prime economic factors are GDP growth rate, purchasing power, wage rates, interest rates, skilled manpower availability, etc.

1. **Gross Domestic Product (GDP)**
   GDP is the total value of all goods and services produced within a country's borders during a financial year. It represents the country's economic production and growth. When GDP growth is strong and consistent, business organizations hire more workers, pay higher salaries and wages, and invest more money in business operations. It also indicates that consumers are buying more.

2. **Purchasing Power**
   Purchasing power is the worth of a currency that could be explained in terms of quantities of goods that one unit may buy. Thus, when purchasing power decreases due to extreme inflation, it affects each facet of economics, ranging from reducing consumers buying goods or services, high cost of living, fall in investors' investments in stocks, low stock prices, etc.

3. **Low-Cost Skilled Workers**
   Skilled workers are those who have the skills and expertise to do the job well and satisfy customers. Highly skilled workers increase the productivity, revenue growth, and profitability of a firm. India, China, Vietnam, and Thailand today are the destinations where many skilled workers are available at low cost. The availability of low-cost skilled manpower is one of the major reasons for foreign direct investments (FDIs) in the manufacturing sector.

Likewise, many other economic factors affect businesses. Therefore, companies analyze all major factors while developing their long-term business plans.

Social Factors

Social factors such as traditions, values, social trends, level of education, the standard of living, etc., have a vast impact on businesses. They affect the habits and spending of customers. For example, in developing countries, lifestyles are changing, and people are becoming more health-conscious; therefore, they prefer to buy gym memberships, healthy foods, yoga, and meditation center memberships. Likewise, many other social factors such as quality education, attitude towards investing and saving, work ethics, religion, beliefs, and change in demography impact people's buying behavior. Therefore, insight into these social factors helps firms develop products and services, and marketing strategies.

Technological Factors

Technology has become the main driver of today's businesses. Most business innovations are coming from the field of technology. Technology is utilized in process innovations, business model innovations, product innovations, and cost reduction activities. The rapid technological changes are making existing technology obsolete within a short period. Therefore, the knowledge of recent technological advancements has become extremely important for firms to develop long-term business strategies. Various technological factors such as technology infrastructure, complexity, technological change, R&D expenditure, and adaption to the latest technology influence many business decisions.

Legal Factors

Various legal factors affect businesses. These legal factors include various laws and regulations on taxation, employment, consumers, securities, immigration, health & safety, etc. These laws and regulations affect business operations. Therefore, all business organizations must know the legal factors under which they have to operate their businesses. Following are some most important laws that should be abided by all business enterprises.

1. **Consumer Protection Laws**
   These laws are designed to define legal relationships between consumers and businesses and protect consumers from any kind of fraud from business firms.

2. **Organization Laws**
   While registering the company, it is mandatory to define its types such as proprietorship, partnership, limited liability partnership, or limited liability company. These entities decide the scope of activities that an organization can perform.

3. **Employment Laws**
   These laws protect the interests of employees against any illegal impositions from the employer.

4. **Securities Laws**
   Securities are the financial instruments developed to raise money from investors. The securities laws regulate the issuance, sales, and purchase of securities. In addition, they protect the investors against any financial fraud from the organizations issuing securities or the middlemen handling the transactions.

5. **Health & Safety Laws**
   These laws enforce health & safety standards at the workplace, such as fire safety systems, noise pollution, air pollution, safety clothing, and so on.

6. **Taxation**
   Tax regulations in the country affect businesses in terms of the cost of production, selling price, profit calculations, exports, and imports. Some countries are trying to develop themselves as tax havens so that multinational giants should come and set up their businesses.

Environmental Factors

Various phenomena happening in our earth's biological, chemical, and physical environments greatly impact businesses. Therefore, we cannot ignore environmental factors while framing the business strategy. The relationship between humans, other living organisms, air, soil, and water is defined by ecology. Certainly, our industrial activities are affecting the ecological balance. As a result, we face problems of climate change, rising waste materials, water pollution, air pollution, rapid depletion of natural resources, deforestation, etc. Because of all these phenomena, there are various environmental issues such as scarcity of drinking water, global warming, deglaciation, increased carbon dioxide concentration in the atmosphere, low rainfalls, depletion of the underground water table, rise in mean sea level, and extinction of many plants, and other living species. Now business organizations are strictly under obligation to follow environmental protection laws to maintain sustainable development.

For example, many beverage plants are using underground water for producing beverages, but in the process, all the nearby underground water tables are sinking deeper and deeper and finally getting dry. It is the responsibility of beverage plants to use appropriate technology for recycling water, rainwater harvesting, and other water conservation systems. Many industrial plants emit a huge amount of carbon dioxide into the earth's atmosphere, cutting the trees to use the woods and land as a resource for industrial activities. These industries are obligated to invest money in afforestation projects, non-conventional energy generation projects, and recycled engineered boards instead of fresh wood. These industries are also releasing hazardous chemicals into the water bodies. They need to build water treatment plants and water recycling plants to save water bodies.

Likewise, many other industrial activities are degrading our environment. They need to reduce carbon and other gas emissions to save the atmosphere, which is the main source of life on this planet. That is why before starting a business or designing any product or service, we need to take care of related environmental factors. For example, suppose we want to establish a hotel. In that case, we must provide a water recycling plant, rainwater harvesting system, other water conservation systems, solar panels, and recycling of waste material, etc.

Swedish furniture manufacturing company **IKEA** is now using rice straws to make its furniture. Rice straw is a rice harvesting residue that is of no use, and that is why farmers traditionally burn it, which creates heavy air pollution. Now Indian oil companies are extracting ethanol from these rise straws. By 2026, Indian cars will run completely on 100% ethanol.

NIKE is the world's renowned shoe and apparel company, which designs, develops, and sells various products for athletes, fitness freaks, players playing basketball and soccer (football), and people involved in other action sports. It manufactures yarns from plastic bottles, which are used to manufacture Nike T-Shirts. In addition, Nike manufactures Air Soles, and its air manufacturing facilities divert more than 50 million pounds of manufacturing waste material per year from landfills. Using recycled material provides a competitive advantage and appreciation from the government and society.

2.3 Five Forces Analysis

Figure 2.3: Five Forces Analysis

An industry is a group of companies producing similar or related goods and services within an economy. There are many forces like suppliers, buyers, competitors, etc., which are affecting the business within the industry. To understand the dynamics of these forces and how these key competitive forces are affecting the businesses within an industry, in 1979, Michael Porter developed the Five Forces Model. These five forces are shaping the competition within the industry. The diagrammatic representation of the five forces model is shown in figure 2.3.

Because of these five main forces within the industry, some companies earn higher profits, and some companies earn lower profits even if the industry is growing rapidly. The major reason behind this earning disparity is the company's interplay with the industry's five forces. The five major forces within any industry are the Bargaining power of suppliers; the Bargaining power of buyers; Barriers to entry, Threats of substitutes; and Competitive rivalry among the firms operating within the industry.

Bargaining Power of Suppliers

In any industry, various business enterprises are operating in a supply chain. A business enterprise becomes a buyer when it buys raw materials or components from other firms to manufacture its finished products. The same enterprise becomes a supplier when it sells its finished products to other organizations such as distributors and retailers or sells directly to final consumers. These final consumers may be institutions or individual customers. In the same way, distributors or retailers become buyers while buying products from manufacturers and become suppliers while selling the same products to final consumers.

To get quality raw materials, components, or goods at the lowest possible price and timely supply in the right quantity, buyers always want to keep the bargaining power of suppliers as low as possible. The bargaining power of suppliers increases due to various reasons, which are narrated in the following bulleted points:

- **Few Suppliers:** The number of suppliers is very few in the industry, and the buyers do not have many options to switch to other suppliers.
- **High Switching Cost to Buyers:** Switching costs arise when a buyer switches from one supplier to another. Switching costs may not be just a financial cost, there may be other intangibles such as convenience.

In some business agreements, there is a clause for **exit fees**. For example, in mutual funds, or banks' fixed deposits, if any investor wants to redeem his money before the agreed period, then he must pay some percentage of gained interest in the form of exit fees. In mutual funds, we call it exit load.

In other business situations **learning cost** is switching cost. For example, if any airline switches from one aircraft company to another, it must provide training to its pilots, crew members, maintenance staff, maintenance engineers, and mechanics. In this situation, another switching cost is **inventory cost** because they need to change the inventory of spare parts.

In some situations, a new supplier may be located far from the buyer's facility compared to the previous supplier, so the transportation cost increases.

One of the most prominent switching costs is the supply of products in adequate quantity and at the right time. For example, in the paint industry of India, the dealers of Asian Paints Ltd. never switch to other companies such as Kansai Nerolac Paints, Berger Paints, or ICI paints. This is because of Asian Paints' major strength of timely and right quantity supply of products in peak season. In contrast, other companies are way behind Asian Paints in this regard. Therefore, upon switching, the dealer will lose their revenue and customers during peak season because of poor supplies.

- **Strong Brand:** In the Indian paint industry, there is a huge demand for Asian Paints in India. Their brand awareness is extraordinarily strong in all parts of the country. That is why it is quite easy for dealers to sell Asian products with an appropriate margin.
- **Network Effect:** The network effects arise due to multiple manufacturers and users sinking towards a primary product. For example, many mobile manufacturing companies and complementary application developers have gravitated towards the Android operating system because many consumers use this system and complementary apps comfortably. Another reason for the network effect is that many users commonly share the product and have learned the use of the product. For example,

Microsoft's Windows operating system and Microsoft Office software are being used by an extremely large number of users across the globe. These users are comfortable using and sharing Microsoft files. At the same time, Microsoft Office files are also opening on Android phones. Therefore, if a product has a strong network effect, then the bargaining power of the supplier increases almost to the level of monopolies such as Microsoft, and every entity in the market gravitates toward it.

- **Easy Forward Integration:** Sometimes, the suppliers have all resources and competencies to go for forwarding integration, but their buyers do not have the resources and competencies to go for backward integration. For example, Microsoft did forward integration and started manufacturing and selling Microsoft laptops, but other laptop manufacturers do not have the resources and competencies to develop the operating system or other office software.

How to Tackle the Bargaining Power of Suppliers?

To survive in the industry, a firm needs to tackle or mitigate the bargaining power of its suppliers. Following are some important techniques, which are helping firms to tackle the bargaining power of their suppliers.

- **Backward Integration:** Many firms are developing their resources and competencies to go for backward integration. The most visible examples are Netflix and Amazon. Netflix in the entertainment industry was positioned at the end of the supply chain where it was distributing films and television shows created by other firms for the final audience. But now, Netflix is developing its movies and videos in partnership with other firms. In the same way, Amazon initially was selling books published by other publishers and products produced by other manufacturers and was using other logistic firms to transport goods from warehouses to final customers. But now Amazon has invested a huge amount of money to produce goods in collaboration with some manufacturers. It has developed its own logistics facilities. It has also developed a self-publishing KDP platform for writers to publish their Kindle eBooks and Paperbacks for free and reach millions of readers.

- **Dominant Player:** If your industry does not have multiple suppliers, then try to become a dominant player in your industry so that you can go for bulk procurement, which is always valued by the supplier. Also, share the supply schedule of future orders with your supplier. For example, in the last 46 years, Southwest Airlines in North America is always buying fuel in bulk quantities to get maximum discounts from oil suppliers. It also gets many value-added services from Boeing because it is using only one kind of aircraft for its fleet. Today, Southwest has a fleet of seven hundred and fifty-three Boeing (737) aircraft serving 101 cities.

- **Timely Payment:** Timely payment is the strongest tool to build productive relationships with the supplier. Every supplier greatly values timely payments as it is directly related to the firm's cash flow performance. For example, many manufacturing firms purchasing raw materials in bulk have developed a system to clear all the previous month's outstanding within the first week of the current month. On the other hand, dealers, buying finished products from the manufacturers and selling them to final consumers are clearing the payments within the credit days limit sanctioned by the manufacturer.

- **Substitute:** To mitigate the supplier's bargaining power, buyers look for substitute raw materials which can be utilized in place of the original one. For example, electricity generated from coal or diesel power plant can be replaced by solar power; petrol or diesel can be replaced by ethanol and biodiesel respectively;

woods are replaced by engineered woods in the making of wooden furniture; in the coastal areas, the underground and river water can be replaced by de-saline water from the sea; and the fiber pipes are replacing the steel pipes.

- **Recycled Products:** The use of recycled raw materials is another best way to reduce the bargaining power of suppliers. For example, instead of buying raw materials, Nike is recycling the waste material to manufacture shoes. In addition, all mini steel mills are using steel scrap to produce steel.
- **Build Partnership:** PepsiCo has built a productive partnership with more than 24,000 farmers across India who are growing potatoes for it. PepsiCo buys 100 percent potatoes from these farmers to manufacture the Lays and Uncle Chips sold in India. In the same way, nestle has built partnerships with African coffee seed producers in Ethiopia, Ivory Coast, Uganda, Kenya, Rwanda, and Tanzania, to manufacture Nescafe and sell it across the globe.

Bargaining Power of Buyers

Buyers with high bargaining power can squeeze the overall industry margins by pushing the firms (suppliers) to reduce the price, increase the quality of products or services, and provide better after-sales services. This situation arises due to the following reasons:

- The number of buyers is less, and the number of suppliers is substantial. In this situation, if the products are not differentiated, then a buyer can easily switch to other suppliers because of low switching costs.
- In some cases, buyers such as Wal-Mart, Big Bazar, Spencer, etc., are centrally purchasing the products in high volumes for their various stores.

- Buyers' bargaining power increases when several substitutes are available in the market.
- Some large-size buyers have the resources and competencies for backward integration. For example, in the paint industry, various paint manufacturing companies are buying pigments from pigment manufacturers, but Kansai Nerolac Paints manufactures pigments to overcome the bargaining power of pigment suppliers. Now Nerolac not only manufactures pigments for its use but also sells pigments directly to other paint manufacturers too. In the same way, HINDALCO established its power plant at Renusagar in Sonbhadra, U.P. India to overcome the power crisis. PepsiCo has more than 32 farms in India growing potatoes to produce potato chips.

How to Tackle the Bargaining Power of Buyers?

As a supplier or a seller, it is imperative to tackle the bargaining power of your buyers to sustain your business. There are many techniques through which today's suppliers or sellers are either mitigating their buyers' bargaining power or managing productive relationships with them. Some of these effective techniques are given below:

- **Forward Integration:** As mentioned in the earlier texts, many suppliers who have the resources and competencies are going for forward integration. For example, companies are opening their retail stores to sell their products directly to end consumers. Very recently, Asian Paints started Asian Paints Safe Painting Service, under which they are painting customers' houses. Patanjali, originally manufacturing ayurvedic medicines, has opened thousands of Patanjali Chikitsalayas (Clinics) and Patanjali Arogya Kendra (Health Centres) across India serving people with free medical consultation.

- **Supplies:** Timely supply of materials is the most important factor for manufacturing firms. For example, Toyota is maintaining just in time inventory system to keep the inventory cost near zero, and for this purpose, they need the supplies of all the spare parts right at the time of production. Also, supplies in the right quantity and the right stock-keeping units (SKUs) to retailers' shops are important; otherwise, they will lose sales to other retailers due to the unavailability of the product. Buyers do not want to change their suppliers who supply the quality material at the right time and in the right quantity.
- **After-Sales Services:** Quality after-sales services are also a particularly important tool to keep the buyer delighted. We can observe many examples of differentiated after-sales services that hotels, airlines, internet service providers, retail stores, white goods manufacturers, automobile manufacturers, and life and general insurance companies are providing to their customers.
- **Settle Issues:** In business transactions, various issues such as damages, breakages, or wrong billings, come up regularly. Therefore, suppliers must settle all the issues quickly to satisfy the buyer.

Barriers to Entry

Entry barriers protect the industry from the threat of new companies entering it and starting a business. If the barriers to entry are high, then the threat of new entrants will be low, which will help existing companies survive in the industry for a long period and sustain their profits. Barriers to entry increase due to the following factors:

- **Economies of Scale:** In all businesses, the fixed cost is spread over several units produced. The more units are produced and sold, the lesser would be the fixed cost per unit. If the existing firms in the industry are producing and selling goods at a mass scale or operating at higher economies of scale, then it would be difficult for new entrants to match the cost. This, in turn, poses a barrier to entry for new entrants.

- **Distribution Intensive Industry:** In the industries such as paints, cement, and steel, the products are sold through an intense dealer network in all parts of the country. It is extremely difficult to sell these products without the proper support of dealers. The existing firms have the advantage of having a vast and strong dealer network across the country, and the new entrants are reluctant to enter the industry because of this very reason.
- **Capital Intensive Industry:** Massive initial capital investment is one of the most prominent barriers to entry. Some industries, such as automobile, telecommunication, integrated steel mills, aluminum plants, and so on, require enormous capital to start an operation.
- **Strong Brand:** Strong brands attract the loyalty and trust of customers, which poses a challenge for new companies to enter the business. The most trusted brands in India are Amul, Patanjali, Godrej, TATA, etc., which poses a strong challenge to new firms to build their brands and join the industry.
- **Patents of Product Design or Technology:** It becomes difficult for new firms to enter the market when the existing firms own the patent of the design of the products or the existing technology. For example, patents of helicopter drones, 3D printers, GPS satellites, three-dimensional electrode devices, Bluetooth, and so on are not allowing new companies to come into business unless they buy the patent rights, which of course, is a very expensive affair.
- **Government Policies:** Restrictive government policies are also one of the prominent entry barriers to new entrants. For example, the Indian government has imposed many business

regulations in the country to protect labor rights, the environment, farmers, etc.

Due to these regulations, many business organizations are reluctant to join the industry.

Threat of Substitutes

A buyer's willingness to buy a product or service largely depends on the availability of low-cost or better-quality substitute products or services. The buyers' propensity to switch largely depends on the product's price and performance ratio. New emerging technologies are also the biggest source of substitution. As we have seen in the past, valve technology was replaced by transistors, android technology replaced all other existing technologies in mobile phones, and videoconferencing is mitigating the need to travel and substituting the requirement of airlines or railways. In the current situation, fiber pipes are replacing steel pipes in civil construction. Focal firms should work on their product's price and quality ratio to reduce the threat of substitutes and at the same time keep themselves abreast with new developments in upcoming technologies and changing consumer preferences.

Competitive Rivalry

The competitive rivalry among the firms operating within the industry increases when the number of competitors is high. The size and market share of competitors are almost equal, and the industry growth rate is slow. When the products are more or less similar, such as soft drinks, soap, moisturizers, fossil fuel, airlines, bus services, etc., it becomes easier for customers to switch between rival products, leading to intense competitive rivalry. In some industries such as house construction, the brand identity is weak, and all the builders are giving the same kind of facilities at almost the same prices, the competitive rivalry is extremely high. High fixed cost causes exit barrier to companies, because leaving the industry may incur a heavy financial loss.

How to Overcome Competitive Rivalry?

It is useless to think about any business without competition. No matter how strong your industry's entry barriers are and how low the threat of substitutes is, the competitive rivalry will always be there, and new entrants will be joining the industry regularly. Therefore, we should always search for appropriate strategies to retain our position in the marketplace and keep ahead of the competition. Following are some strategies to solve the above concerns:

- **Identity the Customers' Problems and Provide Solutions with Your Products:** As discussed earlier in strategic positioning, you need to identify the specific problems that your customers are facing and provide solutions to them. For example, in 1972, a more than $30 billion company Nike identified the specific need for lightweight shoes to improve an individual's athletic performance and introduced lightweight training shoes with an outsole with guff-type roots for traction. In 1979, Nike introduced Nike Air technology, which further strengthened Nike's position in the market.
- **Reduce the Cost and Increase the Value in Your Existing Products:** Normally, strategists understand that a value increase in the product will incur a cost. This means value and cost are directly proportional to each other, but according to W. Chan Kim and Renee Mauborgne's Blue Ocean Strategy, there are ways through which you can increase the value and decrease the price of your product or services simultaneously. It is all about creating a new market within the same industry where there is no competition. For example, Netflix has created new demand within the same industry by offering movies, web series, and

videos in a low-price subscription to viewers. As a result, they have created a new market within the same industry with little or no competition.

- **Differentiate Your Products:** To create space in the industry, many firms try to differentiate their products and services from rivals. Successful product differentiation creates a competitive advantage that helps in building brand awareness. For example, the chain of Ritz-Carlton Hotels differentiates itself from other chains of hotels by focusing on personalization. They have created their own space and industry standard by creating personalization in hospitality. First, they create their customers' database about their lifestyle, habits, food choices, likings, and disliking. Then, whenever the customer is entering any facility anywhere in the world, they customize their services according to the customer's choices.
- **Develop Partnerships with Rivals:** By considering rivals as your partner and creating strategic alliances, you can create your space in the industry and get bigger market shares and profits. For example, Sony and Samsung joined hands in 2004 to share R&D costs to design flat-screen LED TVs. Likewise, Ford and Toyota came together to develop a new hybrid vehicle in 2013.

2.4 BCG Matrix

The BCG Matrix was developed by Bruce D. Henderson of the Boston Consulting Group in 1970. This matrix provides great help to companies analyzing their various portfolios, brands, or products, and evaluates their strategic potential. In addition, this analysis helps companies decide which portfolio, brand, or product the company should invest in, and which should be divested. BCG's growth-share matrix holds four distinct categories: Dogs, Question Marks, Stars, and Cash Cows. These categories are evaluated on two parameters, i.e., Market Growth Rate and Relative Market Share.

Market Growth Rate: Higher market growth rate indicates ample opportunity to grow and earn more profit in the long run. But to match with a higher market growth rate and cater to the high demand, there requires a large investment of money for developing production facilities and making marketing efforts.

Relative Market Share: High market share facilitate higher cash returns. The market share of a product indicates its position in the market against major competitors. It also indicates the future potential of a product or a portfolio.

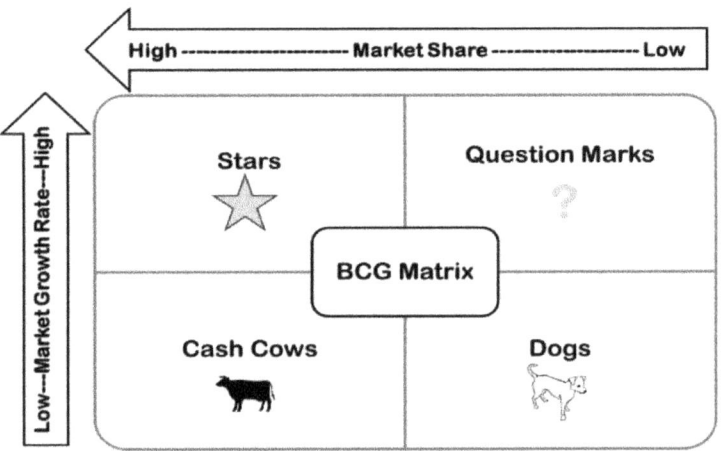

Figure 2.4: BCG Matrix

The Cash Cows: The products or portfolios that fall under this category enjoy their higher market share means higher profits in a slow-growing market. Higher profits are being generated because of the low investments required due to slow market growth. Therefore, companies do not invest in future growth in this category and try to milk more cash from their cash cow products or portfolios. For example, the future growth potentials are low in fossil fuel cars than in hybrid or electric cars.

Therefore, established automobile manufacturers may keep their petrol cars in cash cow categories and milk the cash to invest in the future growth of star products, i.e., hybrid or electric cars. Other examples of cash cow products are Apple MacBook, Apple iPhone, Samsung Galaxy, Jackson's petrol or diesel generators, Toyota's SUVs, and so on.

The Stars: The stars are the products or portfolios that have large market shares in fast-growing markets and have tremendous future potential. These products demand huge investments from the company to cater to the market demand. Therefore, companies should invest money in the products or portfolios falling in the star category. Today the star products for established companies may be solar panels, hybrid cars, electric cars, or 5G technology.

The Question Marks: These are the portfolios or products with smaller market shares in a high-growth market. They consume large cash and generate low cash. Companies are analyzing these products deeply to understand which product or portfolio has the potential to snatch high market share and convert itself into a star or which products are likely to lose market share and turn into dogs when the growth of the market declines.

The Dogs: Dogs are the product lines with a small market share in a mature and slow-growing industry. Usually, these product lines are performing at their breakeven level and just maintaining their market share. These units are worthless in terms of earnings, but some companies continue these product lines to give jobs or maintain the established brand.

Today successful companies are keeping different portfolios of products that fall under the star and cash cow categories. The cash cow category portfolios provide enough cash to the company to utilize for star category products to meet the high demands of the high-growth market.

How to utilize BCG Matrix?

In India, Patanjali Ayurveda Ltd. has many portfolios such as Natural Food Products, Natural Health Care, Natural Personal Care, Ayurvedic Medicines, Herbal Home Care, Patanjali Publications, etc. Patanjali can analyze its different products' portfolios by using the BCG matrix in the following steps:

Step 1: Select a Product or Products' Portfolio: Patanjali can select the entire product portfolio, such as Natural Food Products, or select specific products for analysis. If the entire portfolio is selected, then it should define all the characteristics of the chosen portfolio. For example, the products under this category fulfill the daily food requirements of customers.

Step 2: Define the Market: Patanjali must define the market in terms of the number of competitors, size of the market, various segments and characteristics of customers, the growth rate of the market, future growth prospects of the market, etc. Online industry reports can be utilized to collect the required information.

Step 3: Calculate the Market Share of the Chosen Portfolio: Once a company knows the total size of the market and its portfolio's revenue for the last financial year, then it is very easy to calculate the market share of the chosen portfolio.

Step 4: Place the Portfolios in the Matrix: Finally, the company can put the portfolio in an appropriate quadrant such as cash cows, stars, question marks, or dogs. After careful analysis of current and future scenarios, the company can make investment decisions

2.5 SWOT Analysis

A SWOT analysis is a tool for identifying and documenting a firm's internal strengths (S) and weaknesses (W), as well as external opportunities (O) and threats (T) that exist in the market. Firms are using this information for developing a business strategy to exploit existing opportunities, avoid threats, and get a competitive advantage against rivals in the market.

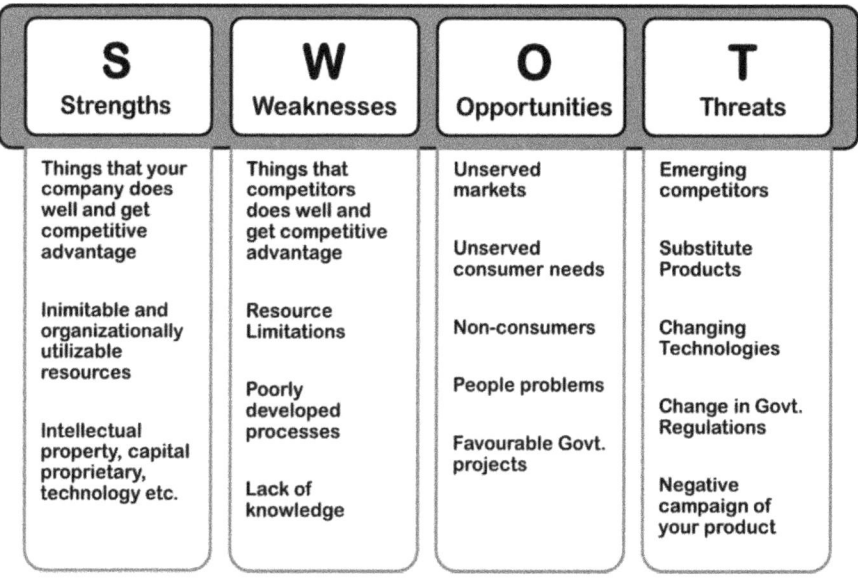

Figure 2.5: SWOT Matrix

A firm's **strengths** are the resource capabilities that provide superiority over competitors. These are processes, events, products' performances, employees' performances, inimitable and organizationally exploitable resources, intellectual properties, capital, and proprietary technologies, which companies utilize to perform well in the market to get a competitive advantage.

Weaknesses are the disadvantages of a firm relative to rivals, such as poorly developed processes, lack of knowledge, and resource limitations. Therefore, the firm's weaknesses are the things that competitors do well and get a competitive advantage.

There are many business opportunities available in the market that a company can exploit by using its strengths. These business opportunities may be as unserved markets, unserved consumer needs, many non-consumers, favorable government policies and projects, and so on.

Certain factors in the market pose **threats** to a firm's business operations. These threats are new emerging competitors, substitute products, new emerging technologies, changes in government regulations, negative campaigns for your products, etc. For example, many health organizations are campaigning against the beverages produced by Coca-Cola and Pepsi, and doctors are suggesting their patients for avoiding the consumption of white sugar.

With the help of the SWOT matrix, the company may take actions such as a change in the business model, change in the process, introduction of new products, mergers, acquisitions, backward or forward integration, partnerships, etc. These measures can help the company to utilize its strengths, exploit opportunities available in the market, overcome its weaknesses and avoid threats arising in the market.

How to Conduct SWOT Analysis?

SWOT analysis can be conducted effectively in four major steps:

Step1: Decide the Objective

Why are we conducting a SWOT analysis? First, deciding on the objective of conducting a SWOT analysis provides the right direction and simplifies our efforts. In addition, it provides insight into the kind of information to be collected from the firm's internal and external environment. For example, the firm's objective may be to introduce a new product, make changes in the process, change the business model, etc.

Step 2: Scan the Firm's Internal Environment and List Major Strengths and Weaknesses

List the things in your firm that you consider your firm's strengths or weaknesses related to your business and objective. For example, suppose you are in the educational coaching business and want to change your business model by shifting to an online coaching mode. In that case, you need to find your firm's strengths and weaknesses related to the coaching business and online coaching. For example, you may or may not have related strengths such as human resources who can develop world-class learning management systems and masterclass course contents, assessments, and related classroom videos.

Step 3: Scan the Firm's External Environment and List the Available Opportunities and Threats.

List various factors which you consider as the opportunities and threats related to your existing business and objectives. Continuing with the same example of the coaching business, you can consider all factors that you may think are related to the coaching business and the online coaching business. For example, covid 19 has opened an opportunity to access a huge number of students for online coaching. After covid, people are now convinced that online learning could be as effective as offline learning. Governments in many countries are now allowing universities to start their online diploma and degree programs. Various accrediting bodies across the world are now ready to provide accreditation to online learning institutions. Business enterprises are also recognizing online certificates, diplomas, and degrees for hiring professionals. Now, these online learning platforms are posing threat to offline learning institutions.

Step 4: Develop Four Types of SWOT Strategies

As shown in figure 2.6, companies may develop four types of strategies from SWOT factors.

Strengths-Opportunities (SO): Using strengths to exploit opportunities available in the business environment.

Strengths-Threats (ST): Using strengths to avoid threats arising in the business environment.

Weaknesses-Opportunities (WO): To overcome internal weaknesses, companies are capitalizing on opportunities available in the business environment.

Weaknesses-Threats (WT): Minimizing weaknesses to avoid threats arising in the business environment.

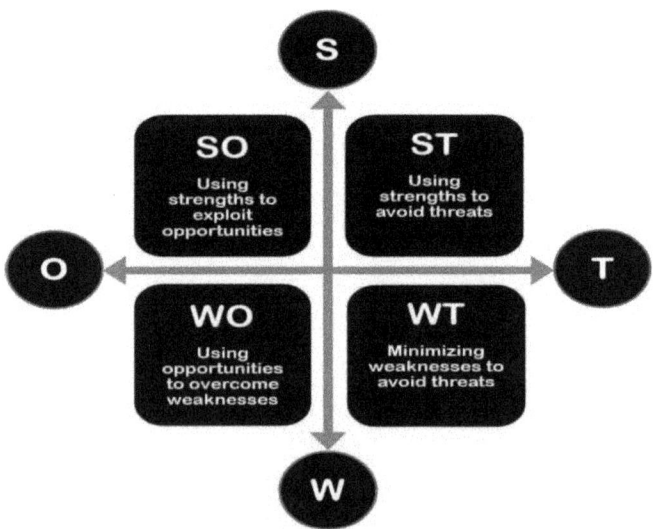

Figure 2.6: SWOT Strategies

After developing four types of strategies related to your objectives, you can use one or a combination of them to achieve your objective. However, the strategies developed from SWOT may not be that effective to get a competitive advantage over rivals. Therefore, we need to augment it by mixing it with other innovative business strategies that we will discuss while discussing different innovative business strategies in the coming chapters.

CASE: BYJU's SWOT Analysis

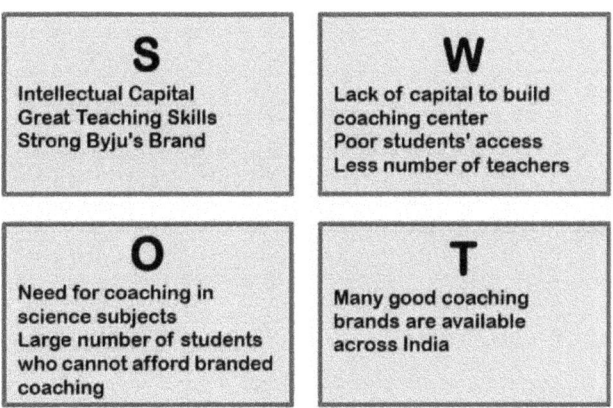

Figure 2.7: Byju's SWOT Matrix

In 2011 Byju founded a company known as "Think and Learn Pvt. Ltd., which is involved in providing science subject coaching to school children, and students preparing for competitive exams in India. Byju himself is a wonderful math teacher. So he did a SWOT analysis of Think and Learn Pvt. Ltd. to access more and more students and increase its business.

Figure 2.7 shows various SWOT factors of Think and Learn Pvt. Ltd. Byju found that the teachers associated with his coaching institute are highly qualified and possess great teaching skills; that is why students are highly interested in joining Byju's classes. There is a strong Byju brand. But Think and Learn Pvt. Ltd. had a fund crisis, and it was not in a position to build huge coaching infrastructures. Due to fewer paid teachers, the firm could not open its various branches in rented premises in different parts of the country. He found a huge opportunity in the Indian educational market as many students want to learn science subjects, and they do not have money to join expensive branded coaching institutes. Think and Learn Pvt. Ltd. also became aware of the threat that there are lots of branded coaching institutions, which are operating in all parts of India. Looking into these SWOT factors, Think and Learn decided to go for online coaching through their videos and online content. In developing videos, they utilized their strengths. By selling those videos and content to a large number of needy students at an affordable price, they grab the available opportunity, overcome their weaknesses and avoid threats from branded coaching organizations.

2.6 Value Chain Analysis

In a business firm, instead of looking at different activities of a business enterprise separately, the value chain looks at a business as a chain of activities. The concept of value chain analysis was given by Michael Porter, who views the chain of activities as a system that converts inputs into outputs purchased by the customers. He divided the chain of activities into two major categories i.e., primary and support activities, as shown in figure 2.8. Therefore, a value chain of a business enterprise is a set of activities that creates value for customers and generates a margin for the firm. The idea behind value chain analysis is to see how different activities perform as a system and add value to each other, improve productivity, and reduce the overall cost.

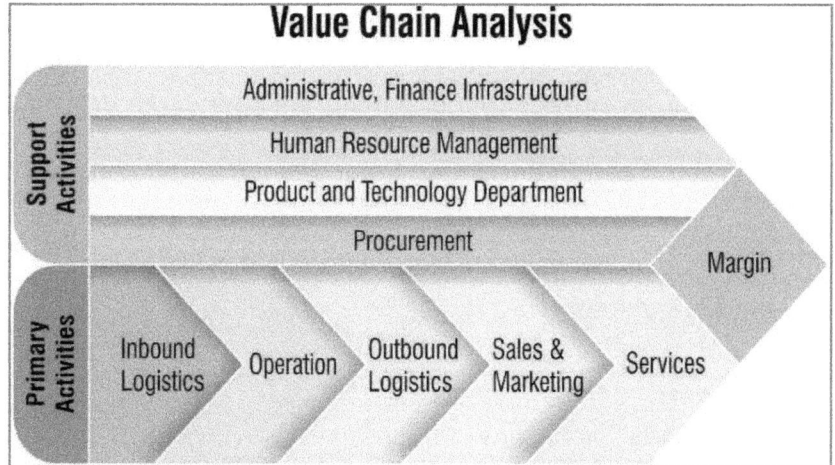

Figure 2.8: Value Chain Analysis

Primary Activities

Primary activities are also called line activities, which are directly involved in converting inputs into valuable outputs, taking that to customers, and giving after-sales services to customers. There are five main primary activities which are narrated as under:

1. **Inbound Logistics**

   The term logistics refers to the movement and storage of goods, which includes the purchase and delivery of raw materials, inventory management, material handling, packaging, shipment, warehousing, and transportation of goods to distributors. Inbound logistics is related to raw material delivery through inbound transportation from suppliers to the company, material handling, and inventory management. The firm's productivity and profitability are greatly impacted by how efficiently and effectively the raw materials are purchased, transported, and stored in the firm's premises until used for production. One of the supporting activities is procurement, responsible for purchasing raw materials, which is inextricably linked with inbound logistics. The timely supply of raw materials in appropriate quantity is key for timely production and fulfilling the demand in the market.

Therefore, while analyzing inbound logistics activities, we should ensure that the entire set of activities is cost-effective, and incur minimal damage and breakage during transportation, uploading, downloading, and material handling.

2. Operations

The operation's activities are concerned with the production of goods and services. For this purpose, you need to organize all required resources such as materials, machines, and labor. Under operations management, you need to make decisions on quality management, location, automation, layout design, process, capacity design, etc. Also, we need to utilize relevant manufacturing technology. The production process is carefully selected as per the product's characteristics, and the number of products to be produced. There are different production processes, such as job production, batch production, mass production, production line, assembly line, or craft production. While analyzing the operation's activities, we should safeguard higher productivity by ensuring that all the resources are organized optimally, the relevant production process is carefully selected and designed, and the most efficient manufacturing technology is utilized. Operation activities are inseparably linked with inbound logistics; therefore, both should coordinate with each other through proper planning, organizing, and controlling.

3. Outbound Logistics

Outbound logistics is concerned with the packaging, shipment, warehousing, and transportation of goods from producers to end-users. On-time delivery of goods in the right quantity to buying institutions, distributors, retailers, or direct consumers is the most important factor for a successful business. Therefore, while analyzing outbound logistics, we should check how to optimize the cost of packaging, warehousing, and transportation and how we can supply the material on time without breakages and damages. Furthermore, outbound logistics activities are intricately linked with sales activities; therefore, proper coordination between the two departments is imperative.

4. **Marketing & Sales**
Marketing activities are linked with all the activities of the value chain. It starts with next year's sales forecasting, upon which the other departments plan their activities. Marketing and sales activities include sales forecasting, communication, promotion, sales transactions, and managing dealer network. With the help of marketing analytics, an enterprise is making decisions on pricing, the amount to be spent on marketing communication, and sales and trade promotions.

5. **Services**
Service encompasses all the activities that enhance or facilitate the sales and use of one's product or service. It embraces the responsibility for making credit arrangements, timely delivery, proper installation, warranty interpretation, and customers' training in the use or care of the product. Unlike direct sales, in indirect sales the salespersons are involved in providing various after-sale services to their dealers, which include a timely collection of payments, settling all the issues regarding wrong billings of unordered products; delayed supplies, and damages during transport; and sales returns; trip and gift schemes; providing account's clarity; and merchandising support.

Support Activities

In a value chain, the support activities assist the primary activities for their smooth conduction so that a firm can get a competitive advantage over its rivals. Following are some important categories of support activities:

1. **Administrative, Finance Infrastructure**
   Under this category, the activities are associated with general administration, accounting and finance, legal and regulatory affairs, and safety measures.

2. **Human Resource Management**
   Activities are associated with recruitment, selection, induction, training & development, and compensation of all the employees working in the organization.

3. **Product and Technology Department**
   Under this category, the activities help develop new products and features, design innovative production processes, adopt advanced technologies, and build appropriate technological infrastructure to facilitate entire value chain activities.

4. **Procurement**
   Procurement entails the activities related to the selection of suppliers and purchasing the material for production.

Steps in utilizing the Value Chain Analysis

Step 1: Identify and Define the Company's Primary and Support Activities

All the activities from the beginning till the end (acquisition of raw material, storage production, marketing, sales, service) should be identified, well-defined, and separated. Different firms may have different value chains. For example, the trading firm is acquiring and stores final products and then goes directly for marketing, sales, and services. They may not require large-scale HRM activities or technological infrastructure. Therefore, each firm should define its value chain according to its scope of operations.

Step 2: Describe the Value of each Activity in the Total Cost of the Product

The total cost must be fractionated down to the cost of each activity. For example, Japanese companies like Sony, Ricoh, and Asics shifted their manufacturing units from China to other Asian countries like Taiwan, Vietnam, and Thailand because the government of the USA puts high tariffs on products produced in China. Each activity has value and cost. Companies decide to relocate, redesign, or replace the activity after doing a cost-value analysis.

Step 3: List the Cost Drivers of Each Activity

By identifying the factors driving the costs, managers can take measures to reduce the cost. For example, if the cost of road transport is higher than rail transport, then managers can decide to transport the material by rail transport. Likewise, if the wage rate of labor is higher in Mexico, then the company can shift its production unit to Vietnam or India.

Step 4: Find out the Total Cost of Linked Activities:

Finding the cost involved in the linked activity is important because reducing costs in one activity may lead to higher costs in the subsequently linked activity. For example, if you start buying raw materials from a distant location because of a lower price, you need to pay a higher cost for transportation. At the same time, the chances of damage during long transportation will increase. The time taken in the procurement of material will also increase.

Step 5: Reduce the Cost wherever Possible

Once the cost drivers and linkages between the activities are established, you can reduce the cost and improves efficiency.

2.7 Resource-Based View (RBV)

RBV is an analysis of a firm's resources. According to Jay Barney, resources are defined as "all assets, capabilities, competencies, organizational processes, attributes, information, knowledge, and so forth of the firm. Within the industry firm's resources are the major reasons for a greater amount of variation in the profitability of different firms. In addition, the firm's resources enable the firm to conceive and design the firm's business strategies and provide a competitive advantage.

As per Dess, Lumpkin, and Eisner, the firm's resources can be categorized into two broad categories, i.e., tangible, and intangible resources. The tangible resources are easily visible in the firm's systems, documents, and assets. In contrast, the intangible resources are hidden and rooted in the firm's rituals, routines, processes, and practices, which are accrued and come to the surface after a certain time.

Tangible Resources

- **Physical Resources:** Land, Buildings, Plants, Machines, I.T. Infrastructure, and other Equipment.
- **Financial Resources:** Liquid Cash, Accounts Receivable, Equity, etc.
- **Organizational Resources:** Performance Evaluation, Reward Systems, Company's Planning, Organizing, and Controlling Processes, Training Facilities, and Procedures.

- **Technological Resources:** Intellectual Property Rights, protection through Patents and Copyrights, and Software Licenses are the Technological Resources, which are tangible.

Intangible Resources

- **Human Resources:** Employees' Skills and Competencies, Interpersonal Relationships, Team Behavior, Inter-Group Relationships, Level of Trust between Employees and Management, and Among the Employees.
- **Expertise Resources:** Technical Expertise, Scientific Expertise, and Functional Expertise in Operations, Marketing, Sales, and finance.
- **Reputation Resources:** Firm's Reputation and Brand Awareness
- **Organization's Culture:** Widely Shared Beliefs, Values, Norms, Attitudes, Routines, Symbols, Rituals, Language, and Ceremonies.

VRIO FRAMEWORK

Barney and Wright (1998) discussed the VRIO framework, which includes Valuable, Rareness, Inimitability, and Organizationally Exploitable organization's internal resources. They developed this framework based on earlier literature, consulting activities, and inputs from executive training. VRIO is a hierarchical framework for determining an organization's success through internal resources.

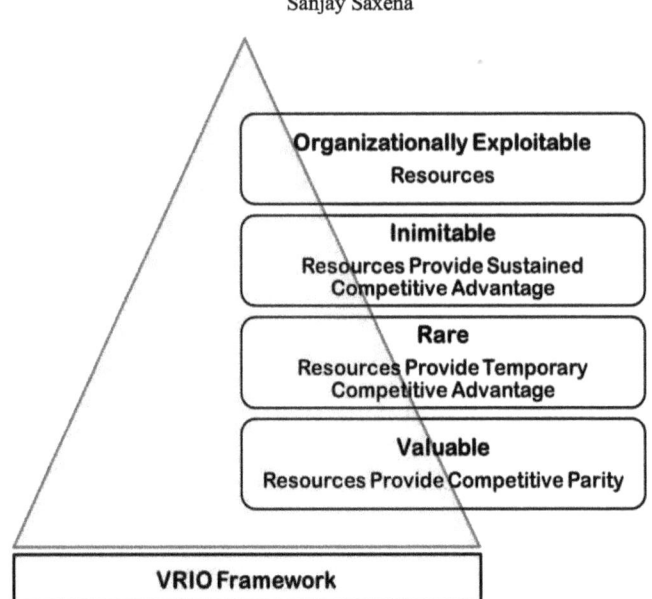

Figure 2.9: VRIO Framework

1. **Valuable Resources**

   The first level in the framework focuses on the question that whether a resource is valuable or not. The valuable human resource allows a firm to exploit business opportunities and mitigate threats from the external business environment. These valuable resources reduce the firm's net cost and increase the firm's revenue. Valuable resources can be procured from somewhere else or developed internally. Internal resources without value are a source of competitive disadvantage. Valuable human resources provide the firm with a competitive parity against rivals.

2. **Rare Resources**

   Rare resources are not readily available in all firms. Only a few firms have these resources. Rare resources could be procured from the external environment or be developed within the organization through brilliant processes and practices. Valuable and rare resources together provide a temporary competitive advantage to the firm. This is because as time progresses, the competitors also develop their rare resources.

3. **Inimitable Resources**

   Inimitable resources are those that rivals cannot imitate or procure from the external environment. Therefore, valuable, rare, and inimitable resources provide a sustained competitive advantage to a firm. The valuable resources get converted into inimitable resources through certain mechanisms, which are as hereunder:

   - **Historical Progression:** Some resources are firmly bounded with the firm historically. They get developed due to the firm's past experiences in adapting to the business environment. For example, In the initial stages, Southwest Airlines faced intense competition from other airlines to manage the operational cost. To adapt to the circumstances, for the first time, they used point-to-point short flight operations between small cities and trained their entire staff (including pilots and crew members) for 15 minutes turnaround times so that they can use the same resources for more flights in a day. These adaptations became their inimitable resource which rivals are unable to imitate. Toyota wanted to reduce the cost of inventory. For doing that, they started an inventory management system of Just-In-Time Inventory, where they trained their entire production staff, procurement staff, and all the suppliers to send the material just in time directly to the production facility. They developed effective software for the purpose. This process of just-in-time inventory became their inimitable resource.
   - **Social Intelligence:** Due to effective transformational leadership and high-performance culture in a firm the employees of the organization start sharing common beliefs, values, norms, and attitudes. Their interpersonal relations within the firm and interactions with suppliers and buyers become extraordinarily

productive. This phenomenon leads to inimitable resources which competitors find difficult to imitate.
- **Network Effects:** Customers are attracted to a product that has better linkages with complementary products or services. These complementary products or services are linked to the primary product because of its large customer base. Also, complementary products amplify the demand for primary products. For example, in India, people prefer to buy cars manufactured by TATA or Maruti because car mechanics and spare parts are readily available in each corner of the country. Therefore, many companies are manufacturing and selling spare parts for TATA and Maruti cars because numerous customers own these cars. Another way of creating a network effect is to create a platform where many consumers have gravitated. For example, Facebook has the accounts of all your friends and persons whom you know; therefore, you will not leave Facebook because you will not find your friends on other platforms.
- **Legal Constraints:** Resources that possess legal protection through patents, trademarks, copyright, and licensing are inimitable and provide sustained competitive advantage to a firm. Replicating these resources by competitors is considered a legal offense, and therefore rivals find it difficult to imitate these resources.
- **Early Mover Advantage:** Many firms get an early mover advantage in converting their valuable resources into inimitable resources. A firm that has entered the industry early has the benefit of learning from its various failures, experiences, and customers' feedback. Then, based on their past learning, they improve their product's design and business processes. For example, Amazon.com came into existence by opening an online bookstore and learned many things about online selling and associated logistics. As a result, today Amazon has

organized its logistical resources most cost-effectively across the world. Unfortunately, rivals are finding it extremely difficult to imitate Amazon's logistics expertise.

4. **Organizationally Exploitable Resources**

According to the VRIO framework, valuable, rare, and inimitable resources are worthless if their organizations do not properly exploit them. Therefore, putting them on the right work and allocating them efficiently and effectively to various events will provide a sustained competitive advantage.

RBV analysis provides insight into various tangible and intangible organizational resources and allows strategists to develop appropriate strategies to convert the resources into valuable, rare, inimitable, and organizationally exploitable resources.

Chapter 3

Strategic Choices (Corporate Level)

3.1 Strategies at Different Levels

Various business strategies are developed and implemented broadly at two levels that are corporate level and the business unit level.

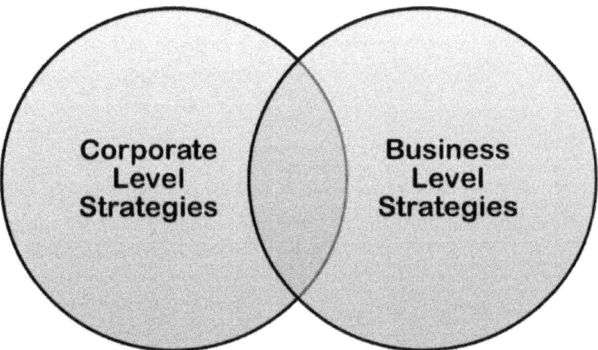

Figure 3.1: Levels of Strategies

The corporate-level strategies are the game plans developed by top management related to the organization as a whole. These game plans address the organization's overall growth and business opportunities in the future. Corporate strategies serve various organizational concerns, such as different business portfolios, product lines, customer groups, markets, etc. These top-level game plans use factors related to the business environment and the organization's internal resources. For example, large corporations such as TATA Sons, Reliance Industries Limited, Godrej Group of Companies, and Patanjali, etc., are making corporate-level strategic choices such as starting a new business division or expanding one of their existing divisions deeper into the market segment, divesting one of their divisions, entering a new market, or starting new product line in the existing market. For example, very recently, Reliance Industries Ltd launched Jio Telecommunications Company. In contrast, small business firms have only a few corporate-level strategic choices such as market penetration to increase profits in the next five years or increasing the market share over the next fiscal year.

The business-level strategies are strategic actions to get a competitive advantage against rivals in a specific portfolio or product category. Business-level strategy choose how to compete in the individual portfolio or product market. For example, Reliance Digital, which is one of the several business portfolios of Reliance Industries Limited sells Realme C11 mobile phones at a low price to get a competitive advantage over rivals. On the other hand, Mercedes-Benz, now a subsidiary of Daimler AG, sells its luxury vehicles at a premium price to premium customers.

3.2 Corporate-Level Strategies

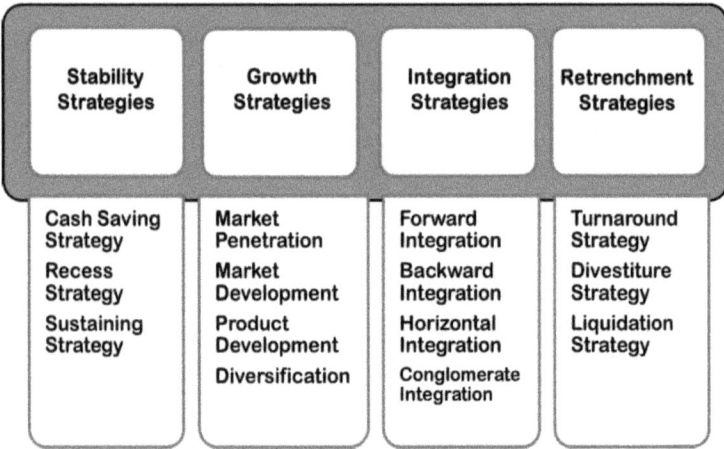

Figure 3.2: Corporate-Level Strategies

As mentioned earlier, top-level managers of an organization formulate corporate-level strategies to provide overall growth to the whole organization. They exploit different business opportunities in various markets. As shown in figure 3.2, there are mainly four major categories of corporate-level strategies as Stability Strategies, Growth Strategies, Integration Strategies, and Retrenchment Strategies.

3.3 Stability Strategies

Under a stability strategy, a firm focuses on maintaining its current market position by relying on its existing products. Stability does not mean stagnancy. No company wants to become stagnant. The firms which are adopting stability strategies want to get along with the industry's steady growth rate in a stable business environment. To get steady growth, a firm concentrate on after-sales services to its existing customers to maintain a steady inflow of sales revenue. There are mainly three types of stability strategies as Cash Saving Strategy, Recess Strategy, and Sustaining Strategy.

1. **Cash Saving Strategy**

   The intention behind no investments in current products and markets is to generate more cash. When a firm has a commanding position in a slowly growing market, it is always preferable to generate cash and invest in other business divisions where the market growth rate is exceptionally high. This strategy is fruitful for the products which are in the maturity stage of their life cycle. The rivals are also not interested in investing in this product category, and therefore a focal firm can easily generate cash and maintain its position in the market. For example, in the automobile industry, petrol engines have reached the maturity stage of their life cycle; therefore, Toyota Motors has adopted cash saving strategy and now just maintaining its petrol engine vehicles to generate cash and invests in hybrid and electric power engines to exploit future business opportunities in the automobile industry.

2. **Recess Strategy**

   A firm is adopting a recess strategy to take a risk-free pause to restructure the organization. The restructuring could be done in various ways, such as rebuilding the board of directors, shifting the power by changing the shareholdings, adopting a new business model, reducing the number of employees, shifting the sales channel from offline to online, etc. For example, many coaching institutions in India involved in giving coaching to students for competitive exams, have adopted a recess strategy and stopped investing in their offline coaching infrastructure as now they are building their online coaching platforms. They have put their coaching business in stability mode.

3. **Sustaining Strategy**

Firms adopt sustaining strategies due to various reasons such as deep economic recession, lack of financial resources, company being under debt or some kind of liability, or the company wanting to go for the merger. In such a situation, firms do not want to take any financial risk and want to maintain their businesses till the situation becomes favorable.

3.4 Growth Strategies

As the name suggests, the growth strategies focus on the organization's growth in market share, profits, number of markets, or business divisions. There are four major growth strategies through which an organization wants to grow its business. These are market penetration, market development, product development, and diversification strategies. The growth strategies are mentioned in Ansoff Matrix or Product/Market Expansion Grid, which H. Igor Ansoff developed in 1957. It was published in the article entitled Strategies for diversification in Harvard Business Review. As shown in figure 3.3, the Ansoff Matrix is based on four parameters, which are existing markets, new markets, existing products, and new products. As mentioned earlier, the Ansoff matrix suggests four strategies as Market Penetration, Market Development, Product Development, and Diversification.

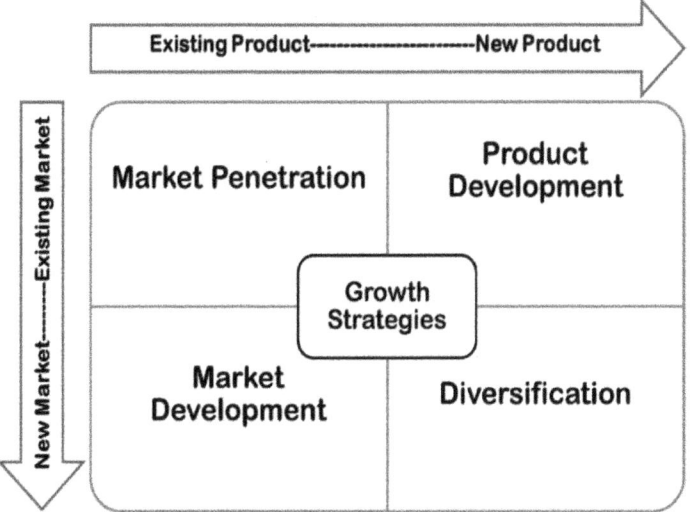

Figure 3.3: Ansoff Matrix

1. **Market Penetration Strategy**

   Under market penetration strategy, a firm penetrates its existing market deeply with its existing product to gain more market share and snatch customers from its competitors. Market penetration strategy carries a low amount of risk as a firm adopting it already operates in the market and knows about it well. Figure 3.4 is showing various techniques that firms are using for market penetration.

Figure 3.4: Techniques of Market Penetration

A reduction in the product price increases affordability and, therefore, attracts more customers to buy the product. Many firms are trying to enhance the value of a product by adding certain new features to it. Innovative product promotion is highly effective to instigate customers to buy. Enriching retailers by making attractive product displays and decorating their outlets with point-of-purchase materials may pull customers to retailers' shops. Opening new distribution outlets in other locations can increase the reach of the product. Opening online sales channels to increase customers' access. Communicating new innovative usage of products is also an important technique to convince customers to buy. Acquiring a competitor firm, building partnerships with a competitor or complementary firms to get more market share, or knocking different customer segments in the same market.

Coca-Cola pursues market penetration as one of its growth strategies. This has been possible for the company due to the incredible strength of Coca-Cola's brand name. For market penetration in India Coca Cola enriched its distribution channels in rural markets, increased its advertising budget during summer, and made partnerships with various restaurant chains.

2. Product Development Strategy

Another strategy to grow is developing a new product for your existing market or improving the existing product to satisfy customers' needs better. The product development strategy requires extensive research and development and expansion of the company's product range. New product development works best when you have a clearly defined problem and a new potential solution. The approach can start from a marketing viewpoint or an engineering viewpoint, but it would be better if you combine people and principles from both disciplines. New product development generally occurs in four basic steps such as idea generation, idea evaluation, product design, testing, and launching a newly developed product in the market.

Idea Generation

Product ideas come from various sources, such as customers, employees, salespeople, channel partners, and the research and development wing. You must generate multiple ideas as there is nothing more dangerous than having just one idea. At this stage, you should collect the ideas without their evaluation. Evaluation at this stage will demotivate people who are suggesting or involved in collecting ideas.

Collecting Product Ideas from Customers

Customer satisfaction surveys and focus groups will tell you what customers think. Instead of asking only about the product features that customers would like, ask more basic questions that will spark their thinking and yours.

- How do you use the product? What do you use it for?
- How often do you use it?

- What would you like the product to do that it cannot do now?
- How does the product fit into your lifestyle or your business operation? What problem do you have with the product?
- What makes it hard to use?
- What do you like least about the product?
- What do you like most about the product?
- If you could change one thing about the product, or service, what would that be?

Collecting Product Ideas from Salespeople and Channel Partners

Ask the following questions to your salespeople and channel partners:

- What are the biggest barriers to a sale?
- How could you sell more?
- What do customers ask for?
- What do they tell you that they would like to see the product or service do?
- What gap do you see in your current product line?
- What do customers like best in competitive products and why?

Collecting Ideas from Employees through Brainstorming

Before generating ideas in a brainstorming session, one has to write the topic on the board. The topic should be written in the form of a problem that is an open-ended question. The open-ended question is a problem statement. Here are a few examples of problem statements:

- What can we do to make this product easier to use?
- How can we lower the cost of producing this product?
- Ways to get more media attention for our company?
- What are the things we can do to solve our customers' inventory problems?

During the session, someone must take notes or better still write the ideas on a blackboard.

There are only two rules in a brainstorming session:

- Participants should mention all ideas that come into their heads, no matter how silly or impractical they seem.
- No one is allowed to criticize or evaluate anyone's idea.

Idea Screening

After generating a sufficient number of ideas, you need to evaluate each idea based on the organization's strengths and weaknesses and available business opportunities in the market. You must integrate similar and correlated ideas and eliminate the ideas which are not fitting to your business objectives and external and internal factors.

Develop and Test Product Concept and Product Prototype

Once the most appropriate idea is selected then you need to develop either the product concept or a product prototype. The idea can be converted into a product concept if we decide its functioning, attributes, tentative cost, and benefits not in a real physical form but at least conceptually. Once the product concept is created then we can present the concept to customers and see how they respond. In concept testing, you gather potential customers' reactions to the product concept. The common mistake we do in product concept testing is that we try to sell it to customers by winning arguments with them. The customer will surrender to your arguments but will never buy a real product. The right way is to ask probing questions and carefully listen and note down customers' true opinions.

A prototype model can be made with anything from building bricks to craft paper. It doesn't need to have working parts—it just gives a rough idea of the design. You can also use computer simulations or working models. Today organizations are developing physical product prototypes with the help of 3D printing.

Design and Develop New Product

Once you convert the idea into a physical form you must consider the design. Design determines how something will look, feel, and work. It also affects cost, materials, safety, manufacturability, storage, distribution, and delivery. All those factors feed into construction, and into how the product will be built. Since people buy design, hence you must concentrate on three major design concerns such as functionality, ergonomics, and aesthetics. By doing a make or buy analysis companies decide about the product's manufacturing. They may go for outsourcing or self-manufacturing, depending upon the cost, scale, and competencies, required for the production.

Market Testing and New Product Launch

Market testing of a new product is inappropriate in industries where the technology requires the same sort of investment for the production of one unit as for a thousand, as in the case of airplanes and cars. On the contrary, the confectionery and beverage industry, for example, can frequently produce adequate quantities of new products for market testing by minor modifications in the production process. Companies such as Coca-Cola or Cadbury, often go for standard test marketing, which is a form of test market in which the company selects a small number of representative cities in which to trial the full marketing mix before a new product launch.

For a successful launch, you must think of the Market, Messages, and promotional mix. You should launch the product to your existing markets with appropriate messages. An effective message emphasizes a reason why a customer should purchase a product or service, and what is the unique benefit of the product or service. In a promotional mix, a company carefully selects the right mix of promotional modes to create a product's awareness and influence consumers' purchase intent. You should utilize various promotional modes such as advertising, sales promotion, public relations, direct marketing, digital marketing, and personal selling to convey a promotional message about the product to the target customers.

3. **Market Development Strategy**

A market development strategy is adopted when the firm enters a new market with its existing products or targets non-consumers in its existing market. Businesses often use market development strategies to identify and develop new opportunities to sell their existing products in previously unexplored markets. You can adopt market development strategies by entering new geographical areas and new demographic segments, attracting non-consumers, and upselling your current customers by finding their new needs. For example, adopting a geographical expansion strategy, in August 2019, a South Korean automobile company, Kia Motors, enter in Indian Car Market with its SELTOS model. They have invested $ 2 Billion in manufacturing Kia cars in India.

A marketing development strategy is important because it helps a business to improve the quality of products or services, acquire new customers, increase revenue margins, build organizational resilience, support long-term company growth, increase brand awareness, decrease production cost per unit, and reach new customers in a planned, structured way. Expanding your customers creates the potential for more leads, more sales, and more revenue, but the in-depth market analysis is essential to make sure that the new target segment is profitable.

4. **Diversification Strategy**

   Corporations using diversification strategies enter new markets with new products or product lines. This involves significantly different sets of skills, competencies, and knowledge. Diversification requires new skills and knowledge and needs to obtain new resources such as new technologies and new facilities. As compared to the other three corporate strategies, the diversification strategies expose organizations to more risks.

   The company can facilitate its diversification strategy by acquiring another firm, developing a new product internally, partnering with a complementary company, purchasing new technologies, importing, and distributing a new product line from other manufacturers, or maybe a combination of these alternatives. There are mainly three types of diversification strategies, as shown in figure 3.5.

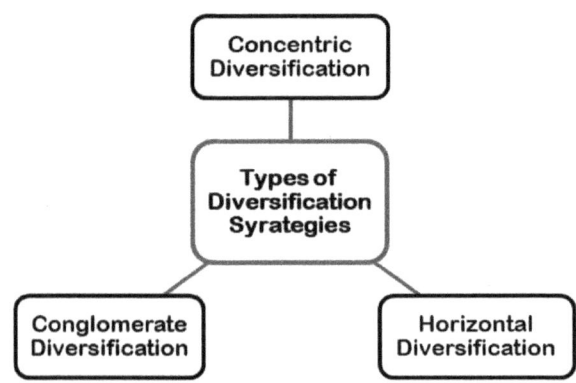

Figure 3.5: Types of Diversification Strategies

i. **Concentric Diversification:** Under a concentric diversification strategy, a firm starts operating in an industry with technological similarities. This means that the firm will gain some advantage by leveraging its technical know-how. For example, in June 2007, Apple Computers entered in mobile phone business with its iPhone. Apple took advantage of its technical expertise in the field of computer hardware and software. Similarly, Patanjali started a new product line of Ayurvedic Cosmetics, in which it took advantage of its experience and knowledge in the field of Ayurvedic Medicines.

ii. **Horizontal Diversification:** The company develops new products that are often technologically unconnected to its existing products or businesses, but that may attract its customers. For example, Kamdhenu Steel entered the paint industry and could attract its current customers. Another way of horizontal diversification is selling unrelated products through the same distribution channel. For example, Nike is selling its T-shirts and tracksuits from its existing retail chains of sports shoes, and woodland sells its Shirts, T-shirts, Jackets, and Trousers from its retail chains of shoes. Other good examples of horizontal diversification are Pepsi and Coca-Cola which diversified from beverages to snacks and selling snacks through their existing distribution channels.

iii. **Conglomerate Diversification:** Conglomerate diversification is a growth strategy under which a firm starts a new company under the firm's umbrella having completely unrelated products or services from the current ones. TATA Group of Companies is an umbrella of the world's most diversified businesses such as TATA Chemicals, TATA Consultancy Services, TATA Motors, TATA Steel, TATA Cancer Hospitals, TATA Salts, etc. Reliance Industries Limited is also a conglomerate giant in India, doing business in the energy, petrochemicals, textiles, natural resources, retail, and telecommunications.

3.5 Integration Strategies

Today, in the business world, the competition is not just between companies; rather, it is between supply chain to supply chain. This is because all products or services are produced and sold by a supply chain. Supply chain activities involve the transformation of raw materials and components into finished products, which are delivered to the end customers through distributors and retailers. Thus, various organizations such as suppliers, logistic companies, focal firms, distributors, and retailers are in a complete supply chain, as shown in figure 3.6.

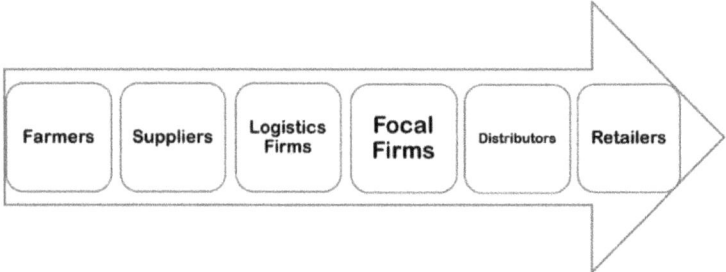

Figure 3.6: Supply Chain Members

To consolidate its position in the market or gain a competitive advantage over rivals, a focal firm may control its suppliers, logistics firms, or distributors through integration strategies.

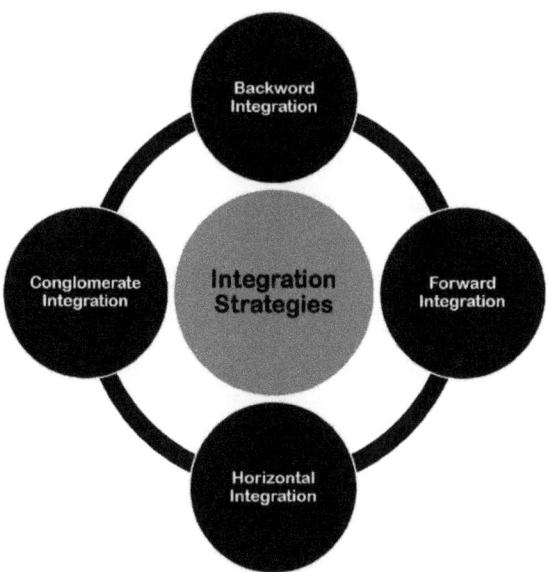

Figure 3.7: Types of Integration Strategies

As shown in figure 3.7 there are four integration strategies: backward integration strategies, forward integration strategies, horizontal integration strategies, and conglomerate integration strategies.

1. **Backward Integration**

   Backward integration is a vertical integration in which a focal firm integrates with its suppliers supplying raw materials or components to it. Also, sometimes it integrates with a logistics firm, which is giving logistical services to it. Therefore, backward integration occurs when a company moves backward to control some portion of its industry's supply chain. One of the greatest historical examples of backward integration is large-scale vertical integration made by Carnegie Steel in the United States. To increase production efficiency, it took over iron ore mines, coal mines, and railroads. Similarly, various companies producing potato chips, tomato ketchup, or coffee are moving back up to commodity producers for contract farming or even acquiring their farms. Companies may facilitate their backward integration through various ways such as acquiring existing suppliers, making partnerships with existing suppliers, making long-term contracts with existing suppliers, or building company-owned supply facilities.

Major Reasons for Backward Integration

Various firms are adopting backward integration strategies to achieve various objectives mentioned hereunder:

- Obtaining control over suppliers and mitigating their bargaining power.
- Getting direct access to raw materials.
- Improve supply chain efficiency.
- Gaining a competitive advantage over rivals through cost efficiency.
- Cut transportation costs and improve profit margins.
- Ensuring the quality of the raw material or components.
- Maintaining the secrecy of technology used in components' manufacturing.

Disadvantages of Backward Integration

Backward integration needs a huge capital investment, which otherwise a company can utilize in other profitable ventures. Also, at the time of economic recession companies will have the burden to maintain additional facilities and employees. After integration, a company may not switch over to substitute components as it must maintain regular purchases from its own supplying units. Normally the suppliers are selling their products to many companies and operate at higher economies of scale, but after integration, many rivals may stop buying from it, resulting in operations at lower economies of scale. Furthermore, if a new supplier enters the market with supplies at a lower price than the company's price, then in that case the company will be in a disadvantageous position. Therefore, further acquiring suppliers will increase the assets and reduce the internal rate of return (IRR) and cashflows.

2. **Forward Integration**

   Forward integration is also a type of vertical integration in which a company moves forward, integrates with, and controls outbound logistics, distributors, or retailers. For example, Nike Inc. the world's leading manufacturer of athletic shoes, apparel, and sports equipment controls its retail stores worldwide. As of May 31, 2020, Nike was operating more than 1096 retail stores across the world.

   Companies may facilitate forward integration with distributors or retailers in many ways, such as by acquiring large distributors or retail chains, making franchise or partnership agreements with distributors or retailers, or opening company-owned retail chains. For example, Reliance Industries Ltd. opens over 1400 company-owned petrol pumps across India. In India, Woodland, Peter England, Raymond, Liberty, and Bata have opened their exclusive retail chains on partnership agreements with various retail store owners.

   Major Reasons to Forward Integration

   A Firm seeks various advantages by adopting forward integration. These advantages are enumerated hereunder:

   - **Increase Firm's Market Share:** By integrating forward, a firm can cut various transaction and transportation costs and lower the price, which helps to increase the market share.
   - **Mitigate the Bargaining Power of Distributor Channels:** By gaining control over distribution channels, a firm can mitigate

the bargaining power of distributors and achieve strategic independence from third parties.
- **Create Barriers for Competitors:** By gaining control over distributors and retail chains, a firm may create barriers for competitors to access existing distribution channels.
- **Better Coordination in Company's Supply Chain:** By having strategic control over distribution channels, a firm can establish better coordination between its suppliers, production dept, marketing dept, and distribution channels. The balance between supply and demand can be created within the supply chain by proper sales budgeting, inventory management at all stages, and regular sales orders from distribution channels.
- **Competitive Advantage:** Due to increased market share, control over distributors and retailers, and distribution access barriers for competitors, a company can strengthen its position in the industry and get a competitive advantage over its rivals.

Disadvantages of Forward Integration

Along with benefits, various disadvantages are also there in forward integration. Therefore, before deciding on forward integration, firms must perform a cost-benefit analysis. If a company finds the benefits of forward integration are convincingly higher than its disadvantages and will sustain it for a long time, the firm should move for it. Following are some disadvantages of forward integration.

- **Huge Capital Investment:** Acquiring or building company-owned distribution infrastructure requires huge capital investment; therefore, the gained financial benefits must be adequately higher than what the company can get by investing the same capital in other endeavors such as R&D, product innovations, or adopting new technology. Acquisition or

investment in building new assets will decrease the internal rate of return (IRR) and obstruct the cash flow.
- **Poor Cultural Synergy:** Acquisition and Merger may be financially viable but culturally misfit. The channels which have their different value system may create barriers to smooth functioning between the two organizations. At the same time, their different value system may affect the services and customer satisfaction adversely.
- **Creation of Exit Barriers for Itself:** By acquiring or building a huge distribution infrastructure and a substantial increase in the number of employees, a firm will have to embrace greater liability, which will create rigid existing barriers for it.

3. Horizontal Integration

In horizontal integration, a firm neither moves backward nor forward. It integrates with a firm operating in the same industry at the same stage of the supply chain. For example, if a firm is a manufacturing firm, then under horizontal integration, it will integrate with another manufacturing firm producing the same products. A firm can facilitate its horizontal integration via internal expansion, acquisition, or merger. In the recent past, an extremely popular example of horizontal integration was the integration of Instagram at the expense of $ 1 billion by Facebook in 2012. Facebook decided to strengthen its position in social media and increase its market share by gaining access to new users. Still, Facebook is operating both firms independently. In 2005 ACC Cement acquired Damodar Cement to operate at higher economies of scale with better productivity. Vodafone Acquire a 67% stake in Hutchison Essar by investing $11.1 billion. Recently on August 31, 2018, Vodafone India merged with Aditya Birla's Idea Cellular, in which Vodafone has a little over 45% share. Aditya Birla group has a

26% share in it. The name of the new entity is Vodafone Idea Limited. Another recent example of horizontal integration is the acquisition of Hotstar OTT Platform by Disney+ in India. After successfully launching in the West world, Disney's popular video streaming platform Disney+ acquired one of the most popular home-grown streaming platforms in the country, Hotstar, and merged its Disney+ offering to become Disney+ Hotstar in India. Disney+ Hotstar currently offers over 100,000 hours of TV content and movies across 9 languages and covers every major sport live.

Advantages of Horizontal Integration

A firm gains many advantages by making horizontal integration. These advantages are elucidated hereunder:

- **Substantial Increase in the number of Customers:** two companies operating in the same industry are more likely to have a separate customer base. After making the acquisition, a firm will get access to the customers of the acquired firm, as has happened in the case of Facebook and Vodafone. Facebook got access to all Instagram users, and Vodafone got access to all Hutchison Essar and Idea Cellular customers.
- **Substantial Increase in Market Share:** The merger of two companies leads to the addition of market shares of two companies.
- **Substantial Increase in Production Capacity and Sales Revenue:** As in the case of the acquisition of Damodar Cement by ACC Cement, the acquiring firm got additional production facilities and a strong market in eastern parts of India.
- **Technological Upgradation:** Sometimes, companies are trying to acquire or merge with firms using advanced technologies. Large multinational giants are always looking to acquire small companies in different countries with special technical expertise.

The acquisition brings the technical know-how of advanced technologies to acquiring firms. For example, in 2006 Walt Disney acquired Pixar Animation Studios by investing $7.4 billion. This acquisition brought new animation technologies, higher market share, and higher profits to Walt Disney.

Disadvantages of Horizontal Integration

Though there are lots of advantages of horizontal integration, no event is free of disadvantages. Some major disadvantages of horizontal integration are mentioned hereunder:

- **Scrutiny from Regulatory Authority:** In the majority of occasions, large horizontal integrations have a major impact on economies, such as a fall in the share prices, or the creation of a monopoly in the industry, and because of that, the interests of customers, suppliers, or employees may get compromised.
- **Reduced Flexibility:** To control a large size organization or to control a large number of employees, bureaucratic procedures get empowered, which in turn leads to inflexibility in the systems and processes, and in adopting innovative approaches.
- **Disharmony Between the Cultures of Merging Organizations:** Each organization has its values, beliefs, attitudes, and behavioral practices. In most acquisitions and mergers cases, strong resentment from employees has been noticed. This for sure leads to the poor performance of the organization.

4. Conglomerate Integration

A conglomerate integration involves an acquisition, merger, or partnership between the firms, making different products, trading in different markets, or operating in different industries. Two firms move into a conglomerate merger to diversify their businesses, increase market share, and create synergy. To form a large and highly diversified corporation, a firm acquires a significant number of unrelated businesses. A good example is Reliance Industries Ltd, in India.

Reliance's Conglomerate Integrations

Aspiring to be among the top 20 companies in the world, Reliance has made several acquisitions in the past. It has invested more than $ 2.4 billion in media and education, retail, telecom, internet firms, digital, chemicals, energy, and space. The companies it has acquired are Embibe, Fynd, Grab, Haptic, Reverie, Saavn, Tesseract, Den Network, Hathway Cable, Datacom, Hamleys, Netmeds, Asteria Aerospace, NowFloats Technologies, Radisys, Balaji Telefilms, and Eros International. In addition, on October 24, 2020, it announced the acquisition of Future Group for Rs. 24,713 crores, which had retail, wholesale, logistics, and warehousing businesses.

Advantages of Conglomerate Integration

Though today conglomerate integration is a rare phenomenon, it has several advantages, as enumerated below:

- **Risk Hedging:** Since a firm gets diversified businesses through conglomerate integrations, other businesses can compensate for the risk of one business failure. Also, all the conglomerate firms regularly analyze their portfolios using BCG Matrix or Directional Policy Matrix and invest in promising businesses or divest poor-performing businesses to mitigate the financial risks.
- **Internal Capital Market:** Capital market is a trading marketplace where financial securities and assets in the forms of bonds, derivatives, commodities, and stocks are bought and sold. The stock markets are a specific category of the capital market, which trades in companies' shares. An Internal Capital Market is a department that allocates capital to various portfolios of the

conglomerate company. The department can alter the allocation if a receiving business is not using the money properly. Therefore, by allocating additional funds, a conglomerate company can revive the sick unit, support the unit to expand and exploit available market opportunities or acquire another business firm to increase market share, customer base, and profits. The allocation of money to different business units majorly depends on their performance. High-performing units are rewarded with a higher allocation to grow further, and low-performing units get lesser funds or may finally be divested.

- **Deployment of Surplus Cash:** The surplus cash available in the company should not be static, and it must be utilized profitably. The best way to utilize this excess cash is to invest it in another company operating in another industry and generate more cash.
- **High Customer Base:** Through conglomerate integration, a firm can cross-sell its products to the customers of acquired companies. This will increase the customer base, sales revenue, and profits.
- **Economies of Scale:** Conglomerate organizations enhance their economies of scale by spreading the costs of R&D, Advertising, Corporate HR activities, and Miscellaneous purchases to several business units.

Disadvantages of Conglomerate Integration

There are various disadvantages of unrelated mergers, which are listed hereunder:

- **Mismanagement Due to Lack of Knowledge:** On most occasions, a parent company does not have technical and functional knowledge of the business of the acquired company, which leads to poor decision-making and mismanagement in the organization.

- **Diversion from Core Business:** Since an organization puts lots of effort into running the business of an unrelated company and in the process, its concentration gets diverted from its core business, and as a result, there is a decline in performance.
- **Cultural Differences:** The merging organizations may have a different set of values, beliefs, and practices. Employees of the acquired organization may face problems adjusting to the new cultural environment. There may be higher employee attrition and a lack of work motivation. For example, in 2014 Google acquired Nest, which was co-founded by Apple's former engineers producing smart home products such as smart speakers, smoke detectors, etc.

This came out as failed venture of google due to distinct cultural differences between the two companies.

Nest's CEO along with many employees left the company after the acquisition because the vision and purpose of Nest were driven by the CEO and were different from that of Google, Nest was more structured in its approach whereas Google's approach was informal, and Nest was a company with a transparent top-down approach whereas Google was more engineer-driven and had a bottom-up culture.

3.6 Retrenchment Strategies

To achieve a stable financial position, organizations adopt a retrenchment strategy to reduce one or more business operations. In addition to the reduction in diversity, an organization may reduce the scale of its business operations. For example, a travel company may decide to pull the operations from less attractive tourist destinations and redirect the resources towards a few destinations, which has the propensity of many tourist arrivals. In the same way, an educational institute may want to run automated online courses to cut the expense of physical infrastructure and teachers. There are three types of retrenchment strategies, i.e., Turnaround Strategy, Divestiture Strategy, and Liquidation Strategy.

1. Turnaround Strategy

The company applies a turnaround strategy on loss-making units to make it profitable again. It is a long-term strategy. Turnaround is a restructuring process that is actualized in three phases: diagnosing the root causes of the failures, developing appropriate strategies, and bringing strategies into action. The main causes of failures are broadly from four reasons, which include economic recession, loss-making products and services, the company's value-chain inefficiencies, and the introduction of breakthrough technologies from a competitor.

Five Cs of Successful Turnaround

A global keynote speaker and best-selling author Skip Prichard emphasize the five Cs for the successful turnaround of a company.

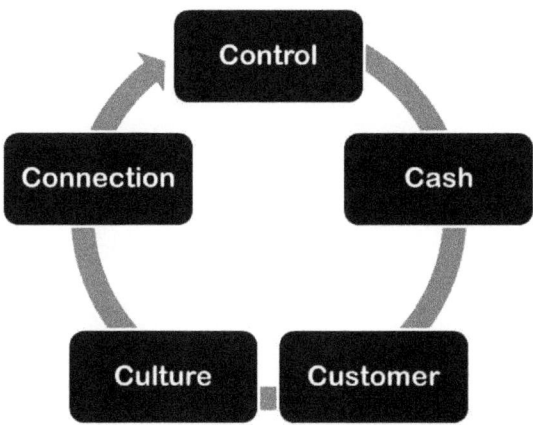

Figure 3.8: Five Cs for Turnaround

As shown in figure 3.8., the five Cs are control, cash, customer, culture, and connection.

Control: Here, control is depicting the centralization of power. In a normal business routine, of course, there must be decentralization of power in the organizational structure, and employees at different levels must be empowered to decide on their domain. But Turnaround time is a crisis time in the organization, and all the processes, procedures, policies, and practices are under scrutiny, and there required quick decision-making. Therefore, centralization of power to the person in charge is imperative.

Cash: Cash is a King. At the time of turnaround, we must look at where our cash is going and from which source the cash is coming, and what is the balance between the cash inflow and outflow. We need to ensure that the balance must be tilted towards cash inflow.

Customer: It has been observed that the managers at turnaround time are mostly busy in deep discussion with their accountants, auditors, attorneys, and other functional managers but what they miss is the customer. In most cases, solutions come from customers' viewpoints. Therefore, turnaround managers should go out and talk to the company's customers in detail.

Culture: Organizational culture is where our employees live every day. Under the turnaround strategy, the improvement in the culture must be given equal weightage along with financials. We cannot implement a turnaround strategy without improving the culture of the organization. Focusing only on financials will not work.

Connection: Here, the connection is related to communication. Turnaround managers must connect with employees, shareholders, partners, customers, and suppliers with effective communication.

Major Strategic Decisions During Turnaround

As discussed earlier, that turnaround strategies are action plans to save failing organizations. It requires quick strategic decisions to turn around the falling trends of the organization. Some of the common strategic decisions are enumerated hereunder:

Cost Cutting: At first, the turnaround managers identify, reduce, or eliminate various cost centers which are non-essential, redundant, and reducible. To reduce the extra cost burden, managers focus on essentializing the inventory level, traveling, hiring, using paper and printing, using electricity, purchasing, advertising, sponsoring events, temporary workforce, and packaging. Some companies follow the practice of recycling and reusing too.

Replacement of Management: The practice of replacing poor-performing management and teams is quite common during the turnaround. This is because the company wants to challenge the status quo and adopt fresh approaches.

Divest Assets: To generate immediate cash, turnaround managers may sell the company's investments, machines, vehicles, facilities, and even the entire business division coming under the dog or question mark categories of the BCG matrix.

Discarding Markets: The company forgoes the business of a specific market, location, or segment. For example, in 1997, Citibank closed its branches in many cities in India. In 2012 New York Life Insurance Company sold its stake in Max New York Life (MYNL) and exited the India venture. In 2007 General Motors declared its exit from the Indian market due to intense market competition and its poor market share.

Discarding Product or Product Line: Company abandons the production and marketing of some loss-making products or the entire product line. For example, in 1998, Apple Inc discarded many of its products that were not selling well in the market. In India, the mineral water giant Bisleri shut down the production of its soft drinks in various flavors such as Pina Colada, Spicy, Limonata, and Fonzo due to non-acceptance from the consumers.

Outsourcing: Reducing the company's assets and outsourcing some of the operations reduces costs, increases the internal rate of return (IRR), and generates immediate cash. In addition, during turnaround time, outsourcing is a better option for risk-free revival.

Layoffs: During the crisis period, many companies may go for layoffs, which reduces some percentage of staff without reducing the responsibilities and tasks of various departments.

Creative Partnership: Companies may go for making win-win partnership deals with other companies in the same industry. For example, in 1997, Apple made a partnership with Microsoft for developing core products. As a result, Microsoft invested $150 million in Apple and started producing Microsoft Office for Apple's Mac.

Innovative Products: The new innovative products are the best source to generate cash and turn the loss-making company into a profit-making company. Companies are always searching for innovative ideas to develop products that can change the company's fate, ss Mac, iPod, and iTunes did for Apple Inc.

Alteration in Distribution Channels: Sometimes, a company gets poor access to its customers because of inappropriate choices of its distribution or sales channels. Many companies are now opening online stores integrated with proper logistics to access a large base of customers. Today companies such as

Microsoft, Sony, HP, IBM, Apple, and so on have online retail stores to sell their products across nations' boundaries.

High-Performance Culture: During turnaround time, a cultural shift is imperative. Transforming the sluggish and fruitless work culture to speedy and high-performance culture is important to generate excellent performances within a short period.

Repositioning: Company uses the repositioning strategy to change the old image and paint a suitable image of the company in the minds of its customers.

Case: Steve Jobs's Strategic Decisions in Apple's Turnaround

In 1997 Apple Computers Inc. was on the verge of bankruptcy, and its CEO Gil Amelio got expelled after 12 years of poor performance. Michael Dell, founder, chairman, and CEO of Dell Technologies said, if he was controlling Apple, he would have shut it down and returned its shareholders' money. But Steve Jobs had a different idea than Michael Dell when he rejoined Apple in July 1997 as interim CEO. Jobs' joining marked the beginning of Apple's turnaround. Steve Jobs took various strategic decisions between 1997 and 2010 and turnaround Apple from the position of bankruptcy to a position where Apple becomes a technology titan. In 2006 Apple surpassed Dell's market cap. Every product released by Apple becomes a guarantee of success. By October 2010, Apple's share price rose from $6 per share (in 1997) to $300 per share. Following were some major strategic decisions that Jobs took during turnaround time:

- **Creative Partnership:** In 1997, Jobs made a partnership deal with Microsoft. He announced a five-year contract that will produce Mac with Microsoft Office. Microsoft agreed to invest

$150 million in Apple. In 2006 Apple made a deal with Intel for using Intel's Core Duo chip technology in MacBook Pro and iMac. This made the system amazingly faster. To again move into software space jobs acquired Macromedia's Final Cut product.

- **Discarded the Project:** He discarded Newton Project which consumed $100 million from a dying company. Also, he abruptly stopped Macintosh Licensing Program.
- **Discontinued Products**: Apple's 15 product lines were reduced to just four desktop and portable Macintosh categories. For the first time, Apple was so lean and thin in terms of the number of products.
- **Distribution Channels:** In 1998, Apple launched a website for the first time to sell its products directly to consumers. On May 15, 2001, Apple opened its Apple Store, which was a brilliant idea. Apple wanted to give proper shelf life and space to Apple products that other retailers were not providing. Through Apple Stores, Apple was able to create a real consumer experience in the stores.
- **Innovative Products:** In a meeting, Steve said you know what's wrong with this company? The existing products are sucking the company, and there is no sex in them. We must invest our resources in new, futuristic, and innovative products. For example, in 1998 iMac was launched, which was a $1,299 all-in-one computer. It came in colorful translucent cases with a unique eggshell design. Nearly 800,000 thousand units were sold within five months of the launch. Later 1,350,000 iMac got sold in one quarter.

After a few months, iPod and then the iTunes app was launched in 2001. With the iPods and iTunes' combo, Apple created a storm in the music industry. In 2005 video iPod was released that boosted the sales of over 30 million iPods. With just iPod and iTunes, Apple generated $10 billion in sales.

In 2007 Apple launched iPhone which immediately revolutionized the telecom industry. Within one year after the iPhone launch, Apple became the third-largest supplier of mobile handsets in the world.

In 2008 Apple released the App Store for the iPhone and iPod Touch. The App store brought 60 million app sales and started generating $ 1 million daily. Steve Jobs mentioned that our App store alone is a billion-dollar invention.

In 2010 Apple launched the iPad using iPhone's touch technology and apps. In the first week of launch, 500,000 iPads were sold.

- **Repositioning:** Steve Jobs' other main concern was to change Apple's sick, damaged image. Through "Think Different" ads and popular slogans, to differentiate Macintosh, Apple promoted itself as a stylish alternative to competitors' computer brands. In 2007 Jobs changed the company's name from Apple Computers Inc. to Apple Inc. This was purely to give a message to the world that Apple is no longer restricted to manufacturing computers only. It is going to produce other tech products that are going to change the lives of people.

- **Cultural Shift:** Steve Jobs knew that it was very important to change the company's work culture to bring every employee into performance mode. He gave the message to employees that he means business and started making hundreds of rejections of ideas given by employees regarding process improvement, product improvement, or new product development. He believed that if you achieve something impossible, you are motivated in a real sense as you have something to say to your children that I was part of the impossible project. Jobs also believed in intense routines of secrecy. At Apple, he created a "closed-door policy" in which employees can enter their authorized zones only. The new hires were posted on dummy positions until they could be trusted. He promoted organizational values such as thinking simply, being different, creating an experience, making tough decisions, taking risks, and great products in better packaging.

Today Apple's market capitalization is more than 700 billion dollars. In 2015 its first-quarter revenue just from iPhone was 51.2 billion dollars, that's more than Yahoo's entire market cap of 45 billion dollars, or three times more than Google's total quarterly revenue, or two times more than Microsoft's total quarterly revenue. Apple has 178 billion dollars in cash, which is much more than enough to buy IBM or buy Ford, GM, and Tesla together. The company has twice as much operating cash as the US treasury. Apple's net income in the last quarter of 2016 was 18 billion dollars.

2. Divestiture Strategy

During business growth, a company develops too many business lines, but at some point, it wants to dispose of some of its loss-making or under-performing business units to focus more on its core business and remain profitable. Divestiture helps the company to reduce cost burden, and debt repayment, focus on core business, and enhance shareholder value. Divestiture strategies recognize the business unit that needs to be divested and why.

Reasons for Divestiture

Various reasons for divestiture are elucidated hereunder:

- **Bankruptcy:** Bankruptcy is a legal petition filed by debtors against a company that cannot pay its outstanding debts. A company is bound to sell some of its business units or some part of its business to clear its debts.

- **Under-Performing Assets:** Due to quality mismatch or economic recession, the demand for a product or product line may weaken, leading a business into an underperforming asset. At this point, the company divests this asset to remain profitable through its other better-performing assets.
- **Closing Some Locations:** In the retail sector, there are some locations where customers' access is much lower than expected. Companies are forced to shut down these locations by selling them off.
- Antitrust Law: These laws are developed by the government to protect the consumers from price-fixing or monopoly and promote fair competition and better services to consumers. Suppose a company becomes too large and creates its monopoly in the market, then the Govt. forces it to divest some of its assets to protect consumers from exploitation.

Types of Divestitures

Companies are making divestments mainly in three forms which are narrated hereunder:

- **Spin-off:** In the spin-off strategy, the parent company makes its subsidiary company a standalone company with its shareholders. Rather than selling shares of the sun-off unit to the public, the parent company distributes the shares to its current investors.
- **Carve-out:** In the carve-out strategy, a parent company sells a certain percentage of shares of one of the business units to the public at the current stock market price. The parent company retains a controlling stake in that business unit. Most companies adopt this form of divestiture because they generate cash from the underperforming business unit and invest that cash into their profit-making business units. Often carve-outs are tax-free transactions in which cash is exchanged with shares.

- **Selling Assets Directly:** Under direct selling of assets, a parent company sells some of the assets (equipment or real estate) directly to another party. This transaction involves cash, and the parent company may get tax liability if it sells the assets at a profit. Normally this kind of divestiture occurs when a company is under intense pressure of debts or wants urgent cash to invest in its growing business units. To avoid tax liability, the company sells its assets below book value.

Divestiture Process

- **Develop Clarity**: The first step in the divestiture process is developing clarity about the divestiture decision. We must give appropriate answers to various questions related to divestiture decisions: why we are going for the divestiture of a specific business unit or a portion of it, which type of divestiture (spin-off, carve-out, or direct sale) would be appropriate to achieve our divestiture objective, what is going to happen with business unit's employees after divestment, etc.
- **Work with the HR Department:** The HR department should develop strategies to tackle employees and ensure that prudent employees should not get into trouble during and after the divestment of the business unit. The HR department should work closely with employees to convince them about their better future after divestment.
- **Work with Buyer:** The seller must ensure that the buyer will run the company and protect the interests of the unit's existing employees, customers, channel partners, and suppliers. In any case, the buyer will not liquidate the business after the acquisition. Once the initial concerns are settled, the seller must negotiate the financials with the buyer.
- **Create Purchase Agreement:** After all negotiations, the purchase agreement should be prepared. The PA must

encompass everything from the purchase price to all the pre-and-post-purchase conditions such as payment schedule, employees' benefits, services to existing customers, and warranties. First, HR must read the entire document in front of both parties. Then, both parties should sign the agreements.

- **Close the Deal:** The deal must be closed by completing all the transactions as per the signed purchase agreement.

How to Deal with Employees During Divestiture

Regardless of the size of the business unit, which is on the verge of divestment, the problems of existing employees must be considered in depth. Therefore, the HR department takes care of employees in the following steps:

- **Identify and Define Core Population:** The HR department identifies the people around the assets under the divestiture process. It's a process of identifying the core population and supporting the population. The core population is closely attached to the functions and success of the asset. The support population is attached to the support function.
- **Ring Fencing:** The HR ring-fences the core population of the asset, which is under divestiture. Ring-fenced employees are communicated by HR that they are being ring-fenced and cannot apply for positions in other units of the company. These ring-fenced employees must satisfy the buyer and ensure that the divested unit is running smoothly after the acquisition.
- **Overcome Employees' Resentment:** Of course, employees will resist being ring-fenced and will have lots of uncertainty in their minds about their future under new management. The role of HR is important here to communicate the reasons and benefits of divestiture. The HR and buyer together must interact with employees and share the vision of their great future. Employees

should be given confidence and assurance about the protection of their interests.

3. Liquidation Strategy

Liquidation is the process of ending the business and selling its assets in pieces to convert all the assets into cash. Liquidation of a business happens when a company becomes insolvent, which means not being able to pay its debts. Liquidation means selling all the assets for cash.

After liquidation, first, the secured creditors will be paid off with the cash generated through liquidation. Afterward, the unsecured creditors will be paid, and if the funds are still left, then the shareholders will be paid according to the proportion of their shareholdings.

Liquidation is not always forced by insolvency. Sometimes voluntary liquidation is also taking place with the consent of shareholders. In this case, the liquidator is appointed by shareholders.

Chapter 4

Strategic Choices (Business-Level)

4.1 Business-Level Strategies

With the help of business-level strategies, a firm wants to satisfy customers better than rivals. To do the same, a firm identifies its target segments and their specific needs and then develops the appropriate strategies to access and satisfy them better than rivals. Business-level strategies are choices of strategic actions made to gain a competitive advantage in individual product markets. The firm's core competencies guide these choices. The purpose of business-level strategies is to position the product in the market based on value and price, which is different from competitors. A firm can achieve this by excellently performing on different parameters or performing differently on the same parameters on which the competitors are performing.

Business-level strategies are developed and implemented to achieve the following objectives:

- To position the products or services in the market differently than competitors based on price and value.
- To gain more sales and profits from the individual product markets.

- To gain maximum market share in the individual product markets.

The strategic choice is not easy, as it is long-term in nature and requires aligning the firm's resources with it. For example, suppose a firm wants to adopt a low-cost strategy. In that case, the firm's entire value chain needs to operate at the lowest possible cost without compromising certain quality standards. Some firms have core competencies in reducing costs out of nowhere. For example, Toyota uses just-in-time inventory with zero inventory cost. Ford motors has an edge over competitors regarding designing and manufacturing car engines, and Kansai Nerolac Paints has strong R&D generating patents for industrial coatings.

As shown in figure 4.1, in the current business environment, various business firms apply different strategies such as Porter's Generic Strategies (Cost Leadership, Differentiation, Cost Focus, and Differentiation Focus), Blue Ocean strategies, Disruptive strategies, and Jobs-To-Be-Done strategies.

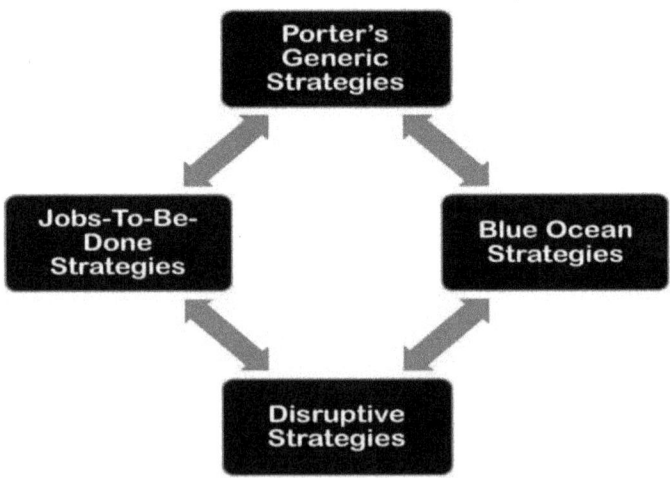

Figure 4.1: Business-Level Strategies

4.2 Porter's Generic Strategies

According to Michael Porter, firms adopt four types of generic strategies to compete in the market. These four types of generic strategies are based on the concentration of two parameters: broad or narrow markets and competitive advantage based on the ratio of price and quality. Figure 4.2. depicts Porter's Generic Strategies.

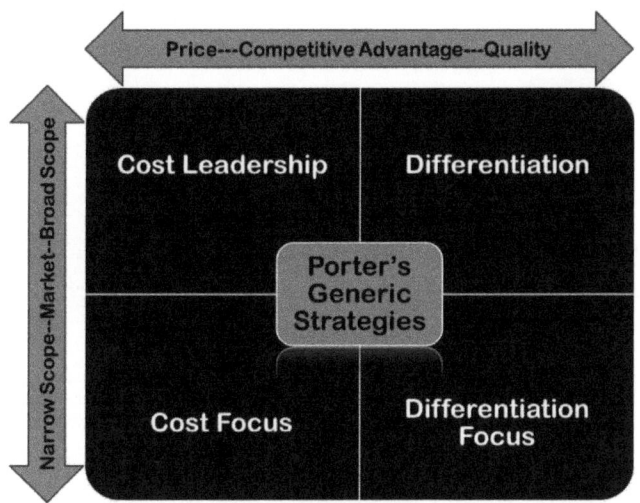

Figure 4.2: Porter's Generic Strategies

Operating in broad or narrow scope depends largely on geography and target segments. For operating at a broad scope, a firm wants to sell its product or entire product line to many segments or across the segments. Whereas in a narrow scope of operations, a firm wants to sell its product to a specific segment. For example, Parle is producing and sells biscuits, snacks, and confectionery products all over India across many segments. On the other hand, a software developing company Bisys is developing software for banks only, and Systematics develops software for universities. Peter England manufactures and sells garments in a broad market to many segments, and Armani is manufacturing and selling garments in a narrow market to a specific target segment.

Companies may position their products based on low prices or with more value-added features at a higher price to get a competitive advantage. For example, MacDonald's has positioned its burgers based on the price lower than its competitors. On the other hand, Emirates Airlines Dubai has positioned its air travel services based on differentiation. As a result, it provides exceptional and premium-class services to its passengers at a premium price.

1. Cost Leadership Strategy

Under the cost leadership strategy, a company produces standard products of a certain quality at the lowest cost and sells them to consumers at a lower price than its rivals. Various firms are adopting a cost leadership strategy to get higher margins and a competitive advantage over rivals. Lowering the overall cost of operations helps the firm to offer the lowest price to customers. For example, the most popular low-cost leader is Walmart, which became the largest retail chain in the world through its cost leadership strategy. Walmart uses slogans such as "Always low Prices," Save Money and Live Better." Walmart offers household consumable items such as frozen vegetables, frozen dinners, canned foods, and so on to consumers at the lowest price. Adopting a cost leadership strategy does not mean offering the product or services at the lowest price by reducing the overall profits. Cost Leadership is all about reducing the overall cost of the company's entire value chain activities and gaining the leverage of reducing the price without compromising the quality and overall profits. Sometimes a company intentionally offers the lowest price for some products with reduced margins to increase its sales revenue and market share.

A low-cost strategy is different from a low-price strategy though both are complementing each other. A low-cost strategy is a business-level strategy in which a company made efforts to reduce the overall cost of the entire value chain. In contrast, a low-price strategy is a functional strategy adopted by the marketing department for various reasons such as penetrating the market, creating brand awareness, increasing sales revenue, or snatching the market share from rivals. For example, sometimes full services airlines such as Air India or Vistara in India offer low price tickets to attract passengers on certain routes.

Benefits of Cost Leadership Strategy

Under the cost leadership strategy, the major goal is to produce goods or services at the lowest possible cost. Therefore, a cost leadership strategy provides many advantages to a firm adopting it. These advantages are elucidated hereunder:

- **Increased Market Size:** Producing quality goods at the lowest possible cost provides leverage to sell the goods at a lower price than rivals. It, in turn, increases the sales revenue and market size of the company.
- **Better Brand Awareness:** As the market grows, many customers come to know about the company and its products.
- **Profitability:** Firms operating at the lowest cost and selling the goods at the compatible price in the market get higher margins and higher profits. A firm gets higher profits even if it sells the goods at a lower price than rivals because of its operations at lower cost, higher sales revenues, and large market size.
- **Business Sustainability:** During a period of deep economic recession, firms operating at a lower cost sustain their operations for a longer duration because of less financial burden.
- **Putting Pressure on Competitors:** Firms operating at the lowest cost can go for an aggressive low-price strategy in the

market and pressurize competitors to sell their goods at extremely low margins or even in loss.
- **Creating Barriers to Entry:** Low-cost operations create barriers for new entrants to enter the market as in the initial phases, they may not achieve desired cost efficiency. New entrants are least attracted to markets where profit margins are low.

How to Achieve Cost Leadership?

As discussed earlier, cost leadership aims to produce the goods or services at the lowest cost or the at cost lower than the rivals. The following methods help companies to operate at the lowest cost:

- **Economies of Scale:** Scaling up the business and level of production brings down the overall cost of operation in many ways. Firms having large-scale production may get higher discounts from their suppliers and companies providing logistics services due to large quantity purchase orders and shipments. The fixed cost spreads over the number of goods produced, and with the results, the cost of production goes down.
- **Using Advanced Technologies:** Using advanced technologies in manufacturing brings down the cost of production, and at the same time, enhances the speed of production. For example, 3-D Printing and Additive Layer Manufacturing Technology (ALMT) impact the aerospace, mining machinery, and automobile industries. The complex digital design is stored in 3-D CAD files on the computer, and a 3-D printer prints the real object using materials such as semi-liquid rubber, plastic, metal, nylon, glass, etc. This 3-D printing provides flexibility to the manufacturer in producing complex designs without using additional equipment. Therefore, a manufacturer can satisfy multiple clients using the same manufacturing facility. Another

good example of manufacturing technology is Virtual Reality. Today designers and engineers are using virtual reality to create complex product models digitally. There is no need to develop a huge prototype. These digital product models are reducing the time needed for designing to manufacturing the product. VR technologies are used massively in the automobile industry. Another new wave of production technology is Artificial Intelligence which allows manufacturers to reduce inventory and operational costs and enhance quality control.

Another example is the Industrial Internet of Things (IIoT). IIoT is the union of many technologies such as machine learning, sensor data, cloud computing, and machine automation. IIoT is used in the predictive maintenance of equipment, visibility of supply-chain operations, monitoring of manufacturing operations, and plant safety measures. Overall, it reduces downtime and increases process efficiencies.

- **Value-Chain Rationalization:** Value-Chain Rationalization is a reorganization of an entire value chain of a company to increase its operational efficiencies. Reorganization may link various primary and support activities, redesigning its various processes to increase production and decrease overall operations costs. For example, various procurement processes, inbound logistics, and operations should be well-designed and properly linked so that the right quality material in the right quantity and price at the right time can be procured. In addition, there must be minimum damages during transportation and storage, along with minimum inventory cost. In the same way, there should be proper coordination between operations, outbound logistics, and marketing & sales departments.
- **Supply-Chain Rationalization:** It means organizing the entire chain from primary suppliers to end consumers into a logical, comprehensive system based on relationships and productivity.

It is the process of systematically evaluating the company's operating network, suppliers, distributors, retailers, customers, and product offerings to find and eliminate inefficiencies and redundancies. The primary goal of supply-chain rationalization is to effectively allocate scarce resources to a company's most productive activities and relationships. To ensure success in the business, each supply chain member must add unique value to the process. During the process of supply chain rationalization, companies focus on various issues. These are like creating a balance between centralizing and decentralizing organizational structure, eliminating redundant suppliers and keeping the optimal number of suppliers, building partnerships with suppliers, supplier certifications, the optimal number of manufacturing units, improving logistical systems through outsourcing, and supplier-integrated manufacturing. For example, under the Supplier Integrated Manufacturing Program, A manufacturing firm invites its suppliers to establish their manufacturing units in the company's manufacturing premises or nearby locations. Suppliers bring their equipment, manage their inventory, and hire and train their workers. In supplier-integrated manufacturing, the transportation and inventory cost is reduced to the minimum.

- **Process Reengineering:** Reengineering redesign and refine various processes to enhance productivity, reduce cost and improve customer service. It builds the process from scratch with the help of systems thinking and technology. It transforms the organization from being slow, unresponsive, and unfocused to focused, responsive, and quick.
- **Henry Ford's Assembly Line Reengineering:** Henry Ford, CEO of Ford Motors, wanted to increase the car production speed and make it more efficient. In their existing production system, the cars under production are fixed at specific locations.

Workers were dragging all the components and parts toward the cars' locations to fit them into the cars. In 1913 Henry Ford installed the assembly line for the first time. In this production system, the cars under construction were moving in a straight line through the locations of various components and parts. This new, improved production process reduced the time of building a car from approximately 12 hours to 1 hour 33 minutes. In this process-reengineering, Henry broke the entire process into 84 discrete steps and trained each of his workers to just do one step.

General Motors Information Systems

General Motors was one of the leading automotive manufacturing companies in the United States. In the 1970s, the automobile market of the USA was facing intense competition from new entrants such as Toyota and Honda. General Motors decided to reengineer the information systems infrastructure to eliminate redundancies, recalls, and warranty repairs. GM incorporated barcodes in all the parts and established a scanning process to identify any missing parts in a car at the end of assembly line work. It helps GM to save millions of dollars.

Lean Management: To keep low operational and administrative costs, many firms adopt a lean management approach. They streamline their organizational structure with only essential layers of hierarchies and the number of employees. To reduce the cost further, they outsource their recruitment, selection, payroll, marketing, and sales functions. In addition, they hire highly skilled young and inexperienced staff at much lower salaries. For example, instead of trained and experienced chefs, McDonald's hires inexperienced cooks and trains them in their food preparation system, which runs on standardized SOPs and is easy to learn. Further, to keep a lean production system and supply chain, McDonald's manufactures and sells a limited range of food products on a large scale.

2. Differentiation Strategy

Differentiation means differentiating a product from similar products available in the marketplace based on newly added features. Under differentiation strategy, a company offers something unique, different, and distinct from what competitors are offering. This unique can be newly added features in a product, product usage experience, buying experience, or after-sales services. The companies are adopting differentiation strategies to distinguish themselves in the marketplace and gain a competitive advantage over rivals. In addition, the companies which are successfully differentiating their products from competitors get the leverage of charging a higher price.

Ways to Differentiate Products

There are various factors through which we can differentiate our products from similar products available in the marketplace. Those factors are discussed hereunder:

- **Quality:** Vertical differentiation is a differentiation based on quality. Quality has a different meaning to different people because quality is majorly a people's perception of quality. But in some products majority of people have a consensus that the product is better than other similar products. For example, people consider iPhone a better-quality mobile phone in comparison to other mobile phones available in the market. Normally the products' quality is measured based on performance and durability of a product. It means a product should perform as per the specifications for a long time without fail. For example, if a water purifier is not purifying the water as per the specifications; then it is not a good quality product no matter if it is exceptionally durable. Further, if the same water purifier purifies the water as per the specifications, but its parts fail in small intervals, the product is not of good quality. The quality of the tires used in the cars is durability and grip on the road.

- **Performance:** Many companies differentiate their products on the basis product's unique performance features. For example, In India, Hero MotoCorp Limited was incorporated in 1984 as Hero Honda Motors Limited and launched its first motorcycle CD 100 by differentiating it based on mileage performance. The company claimed that the motorcycle would run 80 km per liter of petrol. When customers experienced that the CD 100 is giving good mileage on road, it captured the market in a lightning-quick time. Fujitsu General (India) Pvt. Ltd differentiates its O General Ac based on its better cooling performance in a high-temperature climate. Reliance differentiates its Realme 7i smartphone on the foundation of better-quality pictures and smoother play. Its punch line is "Capture Sharper and Play Smoother."
- **Durability:** Many firms differentiate their products based on the length of the product's life. For example, Toyota Cars' engines are exceptionally durable and work efficiently even after running 150,000 km. Apple Inc. also differentiates its products such as iPhones, iPads, or iMacs based on durability. Duracell Battery differentiates itself from other alkaline batteries based on its long-lasting life.
- **Features:** Features are the additional attributes added to products that enhance the product's attractiveness to the consumer. For example, Kia Seltos is stacked with 8-Speaker Bose Audio System. The higher priced laptops are providing touch screen and front and rear-view camera facilities.
- **After Sales Service:** Companies such as LG Electronics differentiate their products based on their responsiveness to customers. Therefore, they offer excellent after-sales services to

their customers regarding product installation, regular maintenance, and quick repair.
- **Aesthetics:** Aesthetics means the artistic, pleasant, or unique appearance of a product. Aesthetics can involve people's emotions and all senses. Apple Inc always puts a lot of emphasis on aesthetics while designing its products. It uses aesthetics both in product design as well as in packaging. Apple's iMac is a classic example of an aesthetically designed product. iMac's beautiful visual appearance attracted customers immediately after launch and became the most successful differentiating factor. On the contrary, TATA Nano's visual appearance could not attract customers. Therefore, aesthetics in product design plays a major role in reaching customers' hearts.
- **Psychological Desires:** Many luxury products such as Hayat Residency Hotel, BMW Car, Rolex Watches, and Exclusive Designer Garments, differentiate themselves to fulfill the customers' desire to have special status, prestige, and the feeling of being a distinctive personality.
- **Wide Range of Choices:** To differentiate their product, companies offer a wide range of choices within the same product category. They satisfy customers by giving them the freedom to choose as per their unique requirements. The wide range of choices may be multiple packings, sizes, flavors, prints, colors, designs, and tastes. For example, Peter England offers shirts in multiple sizes, shades, and prints. Quality Walls sells ice cream in multiple packings and flavors. Revlon offers hundreds of shades in each color category of lipstick.

Differentiation Strategy of Virgin Airlines

Unlike Southwest Airlines which offers point-to-point flights at the lowest fare and limited services to its customers, Virgin Airlines offers full-service flights at affordable fares. They offer boarding passes with seat numbers, baggage handling service, on-plane Wi-Fi, touchscreen seatback entertainment, high-quality, regionally inspired dishes from the flight destination, complimentary beverages, excellent customer service, catering, etc.

3. Focus Strategy

Under focus strategy, companies try to target their products to a specific niche market or a narrow segment of customers. Thus, it is directed toward satisfying the needs of a narrow group of customers. These niche markets can be identified based on the following parameters:

- **Specific Groups of Customers:** The customers can be divided into various specific groups such as women, men, youth, adolescents, rich class, middle class, farmers, senior citizens, etc. For example, Rolls Royce manufactures luxury automobiles for the rich class of customers; Harley and Davidson Motorcycle's target segment is Caucasian males over 35+. On the other hand, Ginger Hotels is a chain of lean luxe hotels in India, which is an ideal choice at an affordable price for leisure and business travelers; Breezes Resorts caters only to couples without children.

- **Specific Geographic Area:** We can geographically segment a market by areas, such as cities, rural or urban areas, countries, regions, and international regions. Under Geographic focus, companies are producing and sell their products to customers living in a specific geographic area. For example, Toyota and other automobile companies produce and sell four-wheel-drive SUVs to customers living in sandy deserts or on mountainous terrains. Companies such as Johnson Outdoors and Sherwood Scuba from the United States, manufacture and sell Scuba Diving equipment in coastal cities located in America, Europe,

and the Middle East. Polaris's manufacture and sell Snow Bikes mainly in snowy regions like the Arctic, Alpine, and the Himalayas.
- **Specific Industry:** When a company focuses its resources on one business only. For example, Asian Paints Limited is the number one paint company in India. It continues to manufacture and sell paint products in Paint Industry only. Subway is an American multi-national fast food restaurant franchise that primarily sells submarine sandwiches, wraps, salads, and drinks. It concentrates and competes successfully only within a single industry to become a dominant player.
- **A Single Product Line:** When a company grows, there is always the temptation to diversify into new product lines. But still, some companies stick to their single product line and have done well in the market. For example, Select Comfort Corporation manufactures and sells mattresses and pillows in its twenty years of business. In the same way, Michelin strictly manufacturing tires for planes, cars, and bikes for many years.

Benefits of Focus Strategy

Companies adopting a focus strategy can reap high-profit margins while remaining small enough to avoid large-scale, head-to-head competition. These companies generate better brand loyalty from their customers because they serve to narrow segments with better quality products and after-sales services. In addition, they can retain their customers better than the companies serving broad segments because their customers cannot find substitutes.

Types of Focus Strategies
Companies use two types of focus strategies: Focus Cost Leadership Strategy and Focus Differentiation Strategy.

- **Focus Cost Leadership:** Companies using this strategy wants to operate at the lowest possible cost in their narrow target segment and offers low price to their customers. They are not offering the lowest price, rather they are offering a lower price than the competing firms within the same narrow target market. For example, Claire targets young women by offering low price jewelry, accessories, and ear piercings.
- **Focus Differentiation Strategy:** Companies using this strategy offer unique features that satisfy the needs of a narrow target segment. A focused differentiation strategy aims to differentiate the products or services from rivals no matter if the product's price is getting a little higher. Some companies following focused differentiation strategy use one specific sale channel. For example, Eureka Forbs do not use a retail network to sell its vacuum cleaner, its own sales personnel sell the product directly to end consumers. Some firms follow a premiumization strategy by offering premium products at a premium price to their narrow premium segment. For example, Mercedes-Benz offers its luxurious cars at premium prices to its premium customers. Another good example of premiumization is Nike, which offers premium quality athletic footwear to serious athletes at a premium price.

Risk Involved in Using Generic Strategies
Despite all benefits, there are some risks involved in using generic strategies, which are enumerated hereunder:

- Technological changes nullify cost advantage
- Uniqueness is not valued by the customers

- Imitation by competitors reduces perceived differentiation
- The temptation to serve many segments dilutes the focus

4.3 Blue Ocean Strategy

W. Chan Kim and Renee Mauborgne have given the concept of the blue ocean strategy. The firms adopting the blue ocean strategy tend to create new markets and demand in the same industry instead of competing for an existing one.

The red ocean is a market space where all the competing firms are confronting and trying to outperform each other by reducing the price or increasing the value of their products or services. But in the process, they are creating a blood bath for themselves. Traditionally, business strategy is intended to beat the rivals and snatch the greater market share from the existing market, but in the overcrowded industries where trade barriers are falling, monopoly or niche markets are disappearing, and existing markets are becoming less profitable, differentiating brands and low-cost leadership are getting next to impossible. Also, under a traditional strategic mindset, it is extremely difficult to simultaneously adopt differentiation and low-cost strategies.

A better solution lies in the blue ocean strategy, which is all about creating your own space or blue ocean in the existing market where there is no competition. Blue Ocean Strategy is all about eliminating the competition instead of fighting with it. Blue Ocean Strategy refers to the formation of uncontested market space that makes competition irrelevant and that creates more value for the customer at much less cost.

In the blue ocean strategy, we

- Create new demand from non-consumers
- Innovate different use of the product
- Eliminate competitors and

- Use both differentiation and low-cost strategy simultaneously so that a company can provide better value at a lower price.

Therefore, the blue ocean strategy is the simultaneous practice of differentiation and low cost that sets off the new market space (blue ocean) in the existing market (red ocean) and creates new demand. The blue oceans are uncontested new market spaces where there is no competition. But despite the awareness about creating the uncontested new market space, most of the firms are unable to create a blue ocean for themselves. Why do these firms struggle to create new markets for themselves? W. Chan Kim and Renee Mauborgne did research almost for a decade to know the answer to this very question.

1. **Common Misconceptions About Blue Ocean Strategy**
   Blue Ocean Strategy is all about creating new market space or new demand, but various firms get trapped in the red ocean and failed to create new markets for their products due to some misconceptions. These common misconceptions are enumerated hereunder:

- **Customer Orientation:** Traditionally, while framing strategy, managers adopt a customer-oriented approach and attract many existing customers to their products. By focusing on existing customers, firms generate better solutions than their rivals but get trapped in the red ocean. But the blue ocean strategy is all about attracting non-customers and dissatisfied current customers. The blue ocean strategy creates new market space by converting non-customers into customers and by again attracting dissatisfied customers. New demand comes from non-customers; therefore, firms must focus on them instead of existing customers.

For example, the initial target segment for the TATA Nano car was married women commuting with their children on two-wheelers. It was a purely non-consumer segment, but later existing customers were targeted at the time of launch. Instead of targeting women driving two-wheelers (non-customers of four-wheelers), all the ads, marketing communication, and positioning strategy tried to convince existing four-wheeler customers by comparing Nano's price and value with other existing cars. As a result, Nano got trapped in the existing red ocean and failed to create a new market (blue ocean) for itself.

Amazon kindle focused on non-buyers by addressing their concern about a smaller number of e-books which are much less expensive and easy to access through mobile or laptop within no time. As a result, Amazon Kindle created a new market for e-book readers, and today it has more than 2.5 million e-titles.

- **Refining Segment can Create a New Market:** Many strategists have a misconception that a new market or demand (blue ocean) can be created by focusing on a market niche. Though niche strategies can be highly effective in getting more sales, they will not create new market space because it attracts customers from existing customers by refining the segment.

Successful market-creating strategies do not focus on refining the existing customers' segment, rather they try to "de-segment" customers (merging two or more segments into one) by identifying commonalities between various segments to generate higher demand. For example, McDonald's focuses on four different buyer groups: professionals who want to eat quick lunch at restaurants, fast-food customers, long-distance commuters who want to take away the packed foods, and mall visitors who want to eat something light. Although there are differences between these buyer groups, McDonald's found some commonalities, i.e., they want quick and fresh, and healthy food at a reasonable price. McDonald's got tremendous success by offering tasty, fresh, and healthy burgers at a reasonable price in quick time to customers from different segments. Netflix created its blue ocean through a de-segmentation strategy and got extraordinary success by offering a vast variety of video content (TV shows, Web series, and Movies in multiple languages) on a common platform to customers from various segments with diverse choices.

- **Every Technology Innovation Creates New Market Space:** The creation of new market space is not particularly about technological innovation. In other words, technological breakthrough does not automatically create a blue ocean. For example, Segway Personal Transporter launched in 2001 was a wonderful technological innovation but failed miserably in the market. It was a self-balancing two-wheeler transporter. You can move forward or backward by leaning towards the front or back. People rejected this engineering marvel because they were unwilling to pay $5000 for a product with some difficulties such as where to park in a crowded place, how to carry shopping bags in it, how to drive on busy and fast-moving roads where sideways are not there, how can you take it on a bus or train, and how can you carry it in your car. The company was sold in 2009. Therefore, we can say that the new market evolves from the value that new technology is adding to people's life.

Value innovation, not technology innovation, is what creates a blue ocean (new market). For creating new markets, technological innovation must be complemented by value innovation. For example, the Uber taxi service app created its new market (blue ocean) not just because of its technological innovation. Its tech innovation was surrounded by value innovation, which added certain values to customers' life as Uber taxis are conveniently available to customers at any location in the city at a reasonable price. It is simple to book and call a taxi through a mobile phone using the Uber app. It is secure because of the GPS tracking system. Various non-customers (people using their own cars) started using Uber services because they can get an Uber taxi anywhere, anytime, and they got rid of driving discomfort in congested traffic, and parking space problems.

- **Market Creation is all about Creative Destruction:** According to Joseph Schumpeter's theory of Creative Destruction, it occurs when a new tech invention displaces an earlier technology or irradicates the existing product or service. For example, the Super Phones (like iPhone 6+ or Samsung Galaxy Note) have a large and comfortable screen and much of the same technology and functionality as a tablet. They are slowly displacing the tablets. Also, we have witnessed in the past that digital photography wiped out photographic film products. In the theory of creative destruction, old technology or products are essentially replaced by new ones. But market creation or blue ocean creation is not always involved destruction. Mainly it involves non-destructive creation wherein new demand is created from non-customers without replacing existing products. For example, in India, Gramin Banks created new demand from non-customers of large banks by introducing microfinance schemes. This microfinance industry did not replace the banks' existing operations.

- **Differentiation can Create New Market Space:** Using differentiation strategies, companies try to stand out from competitors. Under differentiation strategies, firms try to provide higher or unique value to customers than rivals. The trade-off is a generally higher price to customers. Differentiation and higher price can attract existing customers or premium customers but cannot create a blue ocean for a company. For example, in 2000, BMW launched the two-wheeler scooter C1, which was different from other existing scooters by having a full roof windshield with wipers, seat belts, and an aluminum roll cage. It was priced at $ 7000 to $ 10000 against other scooters priced at $ 3000 to $ 5000. Although it created differentiation, it failed in the market as customers were unwilling to pay a premium price. In 2003 BMW stopped the production of C1. BMW failed because it focused only on creating and raising its offerings and forgot about what to eliminate and reduce in its offerings to keep the price lower than the competitors. Therefore, a firm needs to focus on both increasing the value and lowering the price for creating a new market simultaneously.

- **Low-Cost Strategies can create Blue Ocean:** Many strategists think that a blue ocean can be created by offering products to customers at a lower price than rivals. But by this mindset, they cannot create a blue ocean because they only focus on reducing the cost but avoid focusing on creating and raising the values in their current offerings. Therefore, by just offering a product at the lowest price without adding any unique value, we cannot create new market space. Only low pricing cannot provide a sustainable competitive advantage because competitors can change prices instantly, just as quickly as you can. Just fighting on price will trap you in a red ocean. For example, Tata Motors launched its Nano cars at the lowest possible price by eliminating various features and reducing engine power. Still, it failed sadly in the market and could not create new market space because it failed to provide any unique value to customers. On the other hand, in the United States, Southwest Airlines created its blue ocean by providing air travel at the lowest possible fare and unique values such as fun trips, timely point-to-point flights, and allowing the reporting time just 15 minutes before the flight time.

2. Ways to Create Blue Ocean Strategies

In the above discussions, we have identified various ways to create blue ocean strategies that are being elucidated hereunder:

- **De-segmentation:** Blue Ocean can be created by considering commonalities across various segments, which can help us generate wider demands. Amazon Prime Video, for example, provides a large selection of original content, licensed movies, and TV shows that can be streamed or downloaded by its subscribers, who belong to various segments. Recently Amazon added a large new segment of 18.4 million football fans with Amazon Prime Video using Amazon Web Service (AWS). It won the rights to stream NFL Thursday Night Football Games in more than 200 countries. This large-scale de-segmentation strategy by Amazon Prime Video has created a blue ocean for it.

- **Focus on Non-Customers:** To avoid the red ocean trap, we need to focus on non-customers and convert them into customers. Growth comes from non-customers. Focusing on current customers may not create a new market for a firm. For example, Netflix serves its content globally to customers from diverse cultural backgrounds. Recently, to attract price-sensitive non-consumers of multiplexes who belong to the lower middle and lower class in emerging economies, Netflix has introduced low-price plans to access movies only on smartphone devices. In the second quarter of 2020, the company added around 10 million new subscribers. It is now clear to us that pricing against current competitors will not create a blue ocean. Rather, it will put us in a price war. But, on the other hand, pricing against substitutes that non-consumers are currently using may create new market space for a firm.

- **Focus on Value Innovation:** As discussed in the earlier text that mere breakthrough technology may not create new market space. It needs to be complemented by value innovation. On the contrary, value innovation can create new market space without any breakthrough technology. For example, Starbucks is not technology innovation. Still, it has created its blue ocean at the high end by providing the ultimate experience of drinking coffee in a third place outside of home and work. Starbucks, founded in 1971 in the city of Seattle, USA, now has become the world's largest coffee café chain having more than 31000 stores across 70 countries. Starbucks has created wonderful value innovation by providing premium products, ultimate physical ambiance, and highly personalized customer service. It has successfully innovated various coffee beverages, elevated food items, and premium crafted iced teas. When people come for coffee, Starbucks' appealing physical ambiance and great music make them want to stay longer and eliminate all worries and pain. 'Customer Intimacy' is the key service innovation of Starbucks. Its staff makes customers feel at home, remembers customers by their names, and remembers their coffee of food preferences. As a result, loyal customers visit Starbucks 18 times a month. Starbucks' mission statement is: "To inspire and nurture the human spirit – one person, one cup, and one neighborhood at a time." In his book, 'Onward' the CEO of Starbucks mentioned that success is not defined by how big you become. The only number that matters is 'one.' One Cup, One Customer, One Partner, and One experience at a time.
- **Pursuing Differentiation and Low-Cost Strategies Simultaneously:** The creation of the blue ocean breaks the value-cost trade-off by pursuing differentiation and low-cost

strategies simultaneously. Firms trying to create new market space use RRRC (Remove, Reduce, Raise, and Create) model. Under this model, firms remove redundant and unnecessary features and processes and reduce the price for reducing the cost of products or services. At the same time, for differentiation, firms are raising some benefits and creating some unique values for customers.

3. RRRC Model

RRRC model is commonly used to develop a blue ocean strategy. This model suggests the following actions:

- **Remove:** Factors that are taken for granted and increase the cost of operations. Make these factors non-essential and try to remove them from the operations.
- **Reduce:** Factors that affect the operations but not with unavoidable intensity. The cost incurred for these factors must be reduced to a significant level.
- **Raised:** These factors add value and should be increased to a significant level.
- **Create:** These factors are non-existent in the current business operations. Therefore, we need to identify or create these factors and include them to add value.

Case Study: Blue Ocean Strategy of Think and Learn Pvt Ltd

(Byju's Case Study: Rupees 2.00 Lacs FY 2011 to 1430 Crores FY 2019)

In 2011 Byju founded a company known as "Think and Learn Pvt. Ltd with a special focus on school children. He formed a great team of 25 to 30 experts across content, media, and technology to build world-class content. In 2015, he launched BYJU's Online Learning App, and over 3 million children got associated within three months of launch. Today Byju has 24 lacs students as paid users. Byju applied the RRRC model on traditional coaching to develop the blue ocean strategy and identified around nine factors that need to be removed, reduced, raised, or created. Those nine factors are enumerated hereunder:

1. **Coaching Premise:** To run a traditional coaching center, you need a building that can be used as a coaching premise. But the buildings in prime locations are overly expensive to buy or rent and require a huge investment of capital. This huge capital investment increases the cost of coaching manifolds.
2. **Teachers Availability:** Traditional coaching center need regular full-time teachers to teach students which involves enormous recurring expenses and in turn increase the cost of coaching. Further, a greater number of students require a larger number of teachers.
3. **High Price:** Due to overly expensive coaching premises and many teachers' requirements, traditional coaching becomes high-priced.
4. **Repeat Classes:** In traditional coaching, it is difficult to repeat the classes for students regularly, teachers keep the repeat classes at the end of the semester just to refresh students about what all being taught in earlier classes, but these are not enough for students who not being able to keep the same pace of learning. In online coaching, students can watch videos several times.
5. **Wide range of topics:** Due to a limited number of classes in an academic session, it is difficult to teach a large range of topics in-depth in traditional coaching.
6. **Students Access:** In traditional coaching, the location of the coaching premises is fixed in a city. To attend the classes, students need to commute to the location every day. The students living in faraway locations cannot join the coaching for this very

reason. Also, many students do not get admission due to the limited number of seats in the classrooms.

7. **Use of Animation:** In the regular classroom, it is difficult to use animation technology.
8. **Learning at Own Timing:** In traditional coaching, the timing of the classes is fixed, and if you fail to attend a class as per the schedule, you will not get the repeat class.
9. **Learning at Own Pace:** Because of limited time and fixed class schedule, every teacher teaches the subjects at some pace that some students cannot get along with.

Following table 4.1. of the traditional coaching center indicates the presence and absence of all nine RRRC factors discussed in the above texts.

Traditional Coaching Center	
Factors adding Cost and Value	**Existence**
1. Need for Coaching Premise	Exists and incurs high cost
2. Teachers' availability in the class	Needed and incur a high recurring cost
3. Price	The high price is due to the requirement for coaching premises and a large number of teachers
4. Repeat Classes	Only refresher classes are available at the end of the academic session.
5. Wide Range of Topics	Only a fixed range of topics are taught in detail.
6. Students' Access	Limited students' access
7. Use of Animation	Almost None
8. Learning at Own Timing	Fixed Time Schedule

| 9. Learning at Own Pace | Fixed Pace |

Table 4.1: Existence of RRRC Factors in Traditional Coaching Center

Byju applied the RRRC model on these nine factors to create a blue ocean for Online Coaching App from Think and Learn Pvt Ltd. The RRRC model of Byju's online coaching is compiled in table 4.2. Byju created blue ocean for his company Think and Learn Pvt Ltd in 2015 and got exceptional success.

Byju's Online Coaching App (Blue Ocean Strategy)	
Factors Adding Cost and Value	**Existence**
1. Coaching Premises	**Removed.** As students can learn online from any place.
2. Teachers' Availability	**Removed.** As teachers are not required when students are learning through pre-recorded videos.
3. High Price	**Reduced.** Due to the removal of coaching premises and teachers' availability in the classroom.
4. Repeat Classes	**Raised.** As students can see the videos any number of times.
5. Wide Range of Topics	**Raised.** As videos covering a wide range of topics are available, and students can watch them anytime if they need.
6. Students' Access	**Created.** As there is no restriction. Any number of students from anywhere can be registered.

7. Use of Animation	**Created.** Animation technology is being utilized in the videos to make things simple to understand.
8. Learning at Own Timing	**Created.** As students can watch videos at any time of their convenience.
9. Learning at Own Pace	**Created.** As students can watch videos slowly by stopping or repeating them in the middle.

Table 4.2: Byju's Blue Ocean Strategy

Now the competition is increasing as new players such as Turito, Vedantu, Toppr, and Unacademy have come into the online coaching space. There is a strong need for another blue ocean strategy to eliminate the competition in the newly developed red ocean of online coaching. Byju has taken a step towards creating a new blue ocean by making a partnership with a reputed traditional coaching institution Akash Educational Services Limited. Only the future will tell about the success of this hybrid model of coaching.

Case Study: Netflix's Blue Ocean Strategy

Netflix started as a DVD-rented company and delivered DVDs to customers via postal services. Then Netflix decided to enter the video streaming market and created a blue ocean for its video streaming market against the movies showing in the multiplexes. They attracted many non-customers of theaters because of higher prices. For creating a new market, Netflix identified around eight factors that are playing a key role in the movie market, which are enumerated hereunder:

1. **Need for Multiplexes:** Initially, for watching movies, you need DVDs and DVD players, or Multiplexes. However, building and maintaining a multiplex is an extremely costly affair. Due to the

requirement of costly multiplex infrastructure, the price of watching movies becomes exceedingly high.

2. **Commuting to Multiplex:** People need to commute to its location and then sit with strangers in the hall to watch movies in the theater. As such, there is no privacy.
3. **High Price:** Due to the overly costly multiplex infrastructure and multiple channel partners in the movie distribution, the price of a ticket goes remarkably high, which many customers cannot afford.
4. **Repeat Watching:** There is no facility to watch the movie again in the theater on the same ticket. You need to buy another ticket if you want to watch the same movie again.
5. **Number of Choices:** The number of choices is just 2 to 4 depending on the number of theaters at a particular location. Also, only new releases are being shown, and for watching old movies, you need to rent or buy DVDs.
6. **Customer Access:** Since there are limited seats in a multiplex, excess customers cannot be accommodated in one show. Due to this reason, the ticket price also goes up.
7. **Flexible Timing:** The showtimes in the multiplexes are fixed, and to watch movies, customers need to reach the multiplex's location on time.
8. **Watching Movies on Mobile:** You cannot watch movies on your smartphone in the multiplex system.

Following table 4.4 is showing the existence of RRRC factors, which are important for success.

Multiplex System	
Factors adding Cost and Value	**Existence**
1. Need for Multiplex	Exists at an extremely high cost.
2. Commuting to Multiplex	Need to watch a movie
3. Price	The high price due to multiplex, channel partners, and limited customers access
4. Repeat Watching	Not available on the same ticket.
5. Number of Choices	Extremely limited.
6. Customers' Access	Very Low
7. Flexible Timing	Not Available
8. Watching Movies on a Mobile	Not Available

Table 4.3: Existence of RRRC Factors in Multiplex System

Netflix got tremendous success by creating its blue ocean in the multiplex movie market, and today its total memberships crossed 195 million in the third quarter of 2020. But now, many competitors such as Amazon Prime Videos, Disney+ Hotstar, Hulu, Zee5, etc., have entered in movies and video streaming market and have made it a red ocean. Therefore, Netflix needs to create another blue ocean in the movie or video streaming market. The following table 4.4 is showing how Netflix has developed a blue ocean strategy using identified RRRC factors.

Netflix's Movie Streaming	
Factors adding Cost and Value	**Existence**
1. Need for Multiplex	**Removed.** As people can watch movies in their homes on a big-screen TV.
2. Commuting to Multiplex	**Removed.** As people are watching movies at home along with their families and friends.
3. High Price	**Reduced.** Drastically down to exceptionally low yearly subscription due to no requirement of costly multiplex infrastructure, no multiple channel partners in the distribution system, and huge customers' access.
4. Repeat Watching	**Raised.** As people can watch any number of movies repeatedly within the same yearly or monthly subscription.
5. Number of Choices	**Raised.** to an extremely large number of choices due to the availability of large volumes of videos.
6. Customers' Access	**Raised to an exceptionally large scale.** Any number of customers can join Netflix from across the globe.
7. Flexible Timing	**Created.** People can watch movies at their house or at any place on their mobile phones at any time.
8. Watching Movies on a Mobile	**Created.** Netflix can be watched both on laptops as well as on smartphones.

Table 4.4: Netflix's Blue Ocean Strategy

Case Study: Blue Ocean Strategy by New Model School

In India majority of parents want their children to become doctors, engineers, or scientists. But getting admission to top engineering, medical, and science colleges is extremely difficult as the competition is exceptionally high. For available 20000 seats, hundreds of thousands of students are appearing in the entrance exams. It's a kind of social status

symbol if someone's child becomes a doctor, engineer, or scientist. Due to parents' aspirations, private schools focus strongly on the quality of science teaching in classes IX, X, XI, and XII, and ignore quality teaching in commerce and arts streams. Parents are also looking for schools which are good at teaching science subjects. Today almost all the private schools in India have made tie-ups with coaching centers (preparing students for entrance exams after school). In classes XI and XII, students are not going to school. Instead, they go to coaching centers to study science subjects and pay extra fees (high price) to these centers. Parents take admission for their children only in those schools which have tie-ups with branded coaching centers. They are happily ready to pay extra huge fees for coaching centers.

New Model School did market research to know how much percentage of students who opted for the science stream to become engineers, doctors, or scientists, got success in their careers. Surprisingly, researchers found that out of the whole batch of students who took the science stream 10 to 12 years back in their schools, only 15 percent of students got real success. Fifty percent of students got very average success by taking admissions in low-rated private engineering colleges paying heavy fees or by changing their streams of study in colleges. The rest, 35 percent of students, failed miserably in their careers. The basic reason behind this high failure rate is that most students have intelligence, instincts, and passion for other fields. Still, due to pressure from parents, peer groups, and society, they forcibly pursue their careers in the science stream.

New Model School also found that many students are not interested in studying science subjects because they want to pursue careers in commerce, arts, fine arts, music, dance, theatre, sports, etc. But no private school is focusing and investing in developing its competencies in these other fields.

With the above information, New Model School decided to create its blue ocean by working on the following factors, which are elucidated hereunder:

1. **Batch Production:** Traditional Private Schools are wrongly believed to produce a batch of students having the almost same set of knowledge, intelligence, instincts, and passion. But according to Howard Gardner, there is multiple intelligence in humans, and in every human being, a different set of intelligence is dominant. Also, every human being possesses unique instincts and passions. Therefore, any effort to try to develop students as a batch is most likely to fail in the future.
2. **Career Failure:** Due to the traditional School's philosophy of batch production, and policy to focus and invest majorly in science subjects, parents' aspirations, and current trends in India, there are many career failures.
3. **Huge Overall Investment in Children's Education:** Due to the two factors mentioned above, the overall cost of children's education is becoming exceptionally expensive day by day.
4. **Identifying Children's Dominant Intelligence, Instincts, and Interests:** For developing the extraordinary career of every

student, it's imperative to identify their dominant intelligence, instincts, and interests.
5. **Nurturing Children's Intelligence, Instincts, and Interests:** Merely identifying the children's instincts or interests will not bring desired results. Instead, the school needs to develop appropriate infrastructure, systems, and culture, and hire expert teachers to nurture children's instincts and passion.
6. **Higher Education Plan:** It's important to develop and execute a higher education plan for students passing out of school. Students must choose appropriate fields of study and institutions after completing their school education.
7. **Grand Success in Life:** If you identify the child's instincts and passion, and nurture them from ten years of age, then it is most likely that a child will get grand success in life.

Following Table 4.5. indicates the presence and absence of seven RRRC factors in traditional Schools that influence students' success in life.

Traditional Schools	
Factors adding Cost and Value	**Existence**
1. Batch Production	**Exists:** The Mindset of traditional schools forces them to produce students in batches having almost similar quality and characteristics.
2. Career Failure	**Exists:** Major percentage of students either failed to get success or get ordinary success in life.
3. Overall Investment in Children's Education	**Very High:** For the traditional way of students' development.
4. Identifying Children's Dominant	**Very Low:** No serious efforts are made in this direction.

Intelligence, Instincts, and Interests	
5. Nurturing Children's Intelligence, Instincts, and Interests.	**Very Low:** No serious efforts are made in this direction.
6. Higher Education plan	**Not Available**
7. Grand Success in Life	**Only a small percentage of students**

Table 4.5: Existence of RRRC Factors at Traditional Schools

New Model School applied the RRRC model on these seven factors to create a blue ocean against Traditional Schools in terms of ensuring grand success for every child. The following table 4.6 is showing how New Model School has developed a blue ocean strategy using identified RRRC factors.

New Model School	
Factors adding value or cost	**Existence**
1. Batch Production	**Removed:** New Model School made its punch line as "Every Child is Special and should be nurtured as per his instincts."
2. Career Failure	**Removed:** There would not be any career failure if you Nurture children's instincts and passion from ten years of age.
3. Overall Investment in Children's Education	**Reduced substantially:** Students having interests in fields other than science need not pursue their careers in science and pay heavy fees to coaching institutions and private colleges.

4. Nurturing Children's Intelligence, Instincts, and Interests.	**Raised Substantially in a Scientific Manner:** New Model School invested heavily in the required infrastructure, hiring qualified teachers, coaches, trainers, and counselors to nurture the instincts and passion of every student right from their class VI.
5. Higher Education plan	**Created:** The teachers, coaches, and parents develop and implement higher education plans for every student.
6. Grand Success in Life	**Created:** New Model School Executed everything scientifically to ensure their students' grand success in life.

Table 4.6: Blue Ocean Strategy of New Model School

4.4 Disruptive Strategy

According to Clayton Christensen, to support business strategy, there are three basic types of innovations, sustaining, efficiency, and disruptive innovation. Sustaining innovation is mainly utilized by established firms to make their good product better and sustain in the competitive business environment along with their existing customers. For example, Apple and Samsung are consistently launching and selling new, improved versions of mobile phones with additional features to each other's existing customers. It helps these companies sustain their revenues and profits, but it does not create new demand, market, or jobs.

Efficiency innovation increases operational efficiency and reduces the overall cost of operations. It helps companies to produce the same product at a lower cost and create better margins and enough capital without creating new demand or market. In addition, it eliminates jobs because of automation and digitization of production processes.

Disruptive innovation transforms expensive and complicated products into simple and affordable ones for non-consumers. For example, Celeron Processor has created new demand, markets, and jobs.

1. **Non-Consumers**

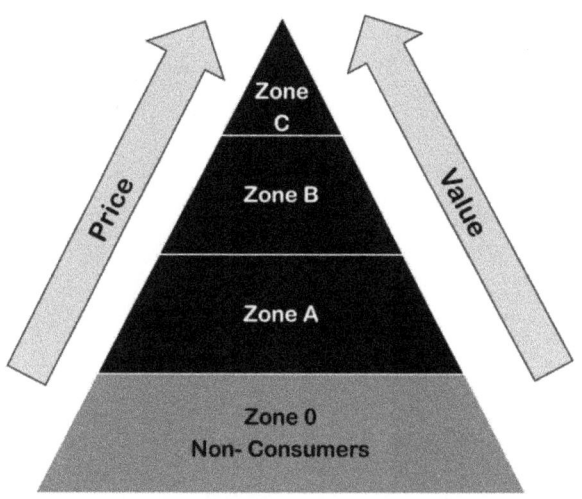

Figure 4.3: Various Products and Their Consumers' Zones in the Market

As shown in figure 4.3, there are various zones in a market where the same type of products with different qualities, technologies, and prices are available for mainstream customers. For example, price and value are increasing from zone A to zone C. But there is also Zone 0 (zero) in a market where non-customers are present. These non-consumers are not buying existing products due to their unaffordable prices or complexity of uses. For example, in the four-wheeler automobile industry, various cars at different prices and values are available in Zone A, B, and C. However, in zone 0, non-consumers cannot buy these available cars due to their higher prices. Suppose a small company introduces a new low-price affordable car for non-consumers, which is of inferior quality than available cars in zones A, B, and C. Surely, it will be something better than nothing for non-consumers.

2. **Disruption**

Disruption starts when a small company that sells its lower-quality product to non-consumers in zone zero in a specific industry, moves upwards to zone A by improving the quality of its product with time. This small company may disrupt zone A by reducing the overall margin and pushing existing companies upwards in zone B. Because of the low margin, zone A becomes unattractive for the existing companies, leaving zone A for a new entrant. In the same manner, Toyota disrupted General Motors in the USA, Canon did to Xerox, Sony with its transistor technology did to Zenith and RCA, Seiko watch disrupted the market of Swiss Watches, and Apple with its personal computers did to IBM.

According to Clayton Christensen who depicted the theory of disruptive strategies, every business has both consumers and non-consumers. Therefore, every business is competing with non-consumers. The disruptive strategy focuses on non-consumers who are not consuming the existing products due to some reasons such as unaffordability, complexity in use, and non-accessibility of the product or service. Disruptive strategies developed on disruptive innovation, which originates essentially at the low end of the market or a new market. Under the disruptive business strategy, 'disruption' is a process in which smaller companies or start-ups with their limited resources challenge already established companies by focusing on the non-consumers and introducing low-quality and low-price products.

Established companies focus mainly on sustaining innovation to satisfy their existing customers by making their good products better. On the other hand, small companies focus on disruptive innovation. They focus on non-consumers at the lower end of the same industry by providing inferior products at affordable prices. For non-consumers, these inferior products at a lower price are like something is better than nothing. Once the smaller companies get the footholds in the industry at the low end, it moves upmarket towards the mainstream higher-end customers by improving their offerings in terms of quality and price. These small companies create disruption when they capture mainstream customers and outcast established incumbents.

In the past 20 years, the theory of disruptive innovation is incredibly useful for many organizations. However, still, most consultants and strategists in various organizations misunderstood the disruptive theory. Therefore, we need to clarify various misconceptions related to disruptive innovation theory to understand disruptive strategy.

3. **Clarifications Related to Misconceptions about Disruptive Innovation**

- **Disruptive innovation is not breakthrough innovation:** In the above discussion, it is quite clear that disruptive innovation is not a breakthrough innovation that makes good products better. On the contrary, disruptive innovation transmute expensive and complicated products into just good enough and affordable products to a larger population, which is non-consumer of it. Every product has non-consumers, and disruptive innovation looks for them and converts them into consumers. Thus, it creates new demand and a new market for small companies.

- **Disruptive innovation does not target mainstream customers unless it achieves the quality level:** Disruptive innovation develops low-cost inferior products for overlooked customers.

Later, through continuous improvement, when a company develops a good quality product, it attracts mainstream customers and disrupts the market. Finally, because of initial inferior products or technology, the established companies overlook new entrants and allow them to enter the industry from the bottom of the market.

- **The established companies should not think of getting disrupted by disrupters:** The established companies should continue focusing on sustaining innovation and keep existing customers satisfied by making good products better. The established companies should start another division to compete with disruptive innovation because it has quite a different operation. Adopting both sustaining and disruptive strategies in the same division will be disastrous, as happened with TATA Nano Cars in India. Tata Motors wanted to offer low-price inferior quality car Nano to non-consumers.

But the company adopted the Nano strategy in its existing division, which was serving its existing customers and failed to attract non-consumers.

Case Study: Disruptive Innovation of KHATABOOK

ADJ Utility Apps Private Ltd. introduced the KHATABOOK App for digital bookkeeping on smartphones. The company was founded by Ravish Naresh, Jaideep Poonia, Ashish Sonone, and Dhanesh Kumar.

KHATABOOK App focuses on small companies and people who want to record their financial transactions (personal or business) by themselves because they cannot afford accountants. At the same time, personally making various day-to-day entries in a physical book is a complex and time-consuming job.

As of August 2019, KHATABOOK recorded over $3 billion transactions on its e-platform. Today KHATABOOK has millions of subscribers across 3000 cities in India, and it is growing 20 percent every week. The KHATABOOK App helps its users by sending WhatsApp and SMS reminders to their clients. It also informs its users about when the money is due to be paid or collected. Having all the accounts ready in their hands anytime anywhere, help people to make better and instant decisions regarding sales, purchase, and giving credits. The app also automatically records all transactions online so that people do not have to worry about losing their smartphones.

To date, KATABOOK hasn't disrupted the market of physical bookkeeping. Still, as discussed earlier, disruptive innovation is a long-term process, and it will take time for KATABOOK to attract merchants and disrupt the market.

Case Study: Disruptive Innovation of Yulu

Picture 4.4: Yulu Bike

Yulu, the bike-sharing solution platform, launched its electric vehicle, Yulu Miracle, in Bengaluru in February 2019. Yulu is currently operational in Bengaluru, Pune, Delhi, Mumbai, and Bhubaneswar. In Bengaluru alone, Yulu has over 850 Yulu zones or parking zones. Users pay a mandatory Rs 10 for a Yulu Miracle ride and an additional Rs 10 per 10 minutes of ride time. First, people use the Yulu app to find the closest Yulu zone where Yulu vehicles are parked. Then, people scan the QR code located on the panel to unlock the vehicle. To end the ride, people are again parking the vehicle at the nearest Yulu zone, locking the vehicle, and click the end button on their Yulu app.

Yulu EVs or their scooters are meant for one rider. It has a 48-volt motor controller and a maximum speed of 25 km per hour, and it requires no license or helmet. A single charge can take the lightweight bike (45 kg) up to 60 km. The scooter of connected to the server, and the company can provide the charge level of every Yulu vehicle across the city. The majority of Yulu zones are located outside the metro stations to provide the last ride to people.

4.5 Jobs-To-Be-Done Strategy

Clayton Christensen narrated the Jobs-To-Be-Done theory in his book Competing Against the Luck, published in 2016. Initially, jobs-to-be-done strategies were referred to as one of the disruptive innovation theories, but later, Clayton develops it as a complete theory in itself. But jobs-to-be-done is intricately linked to disruptive strategies because disruptive innovations are a business model to do business with non-consumers. Disruption theories cannot help us create products or services, but the jobs-to-be-done theory helps us develop unique products or services that perform the jobs for customers. For example, washing machines are doing the job of washing clothes, Yulu vehicles are doing the job of helping people to commute short distances, and OLA taxis or Metro Rails are doing the job of helping people to commute long distances. Thus, the Jobs-to-be-done theory can target both high-end and low-end existing consumers and non-consumers.

The jobs-To-Be-Done theory suggests that customers are the wrong unit of analysis. Understanding the job that a product is doing for customers is important for innovation and not customers. Most successful innovations have focused on jobs that people need to perform. Every product or service must perform some job for customers. Characteristics of a customer can tell us about his propensity to buy a product, but certainly, those characteristics are not the cause to buy. For example, educated people can buy a newspaper, but education is not the cause for buying a newspaper. Collecting more and more psychographic and demographic information about customers and making decisions may take the firms in the wrong direction. We need to develop a product around the job.

There are four principles to understanding jobs to be done which are enumerated hereunder:

1. **Customers' Circumstances are more important than Customers' Characteristics**
   Circumstances and time of purchase are also particularly important. Customers may use the same product for various jobs in different circumstances. For example, in different circumstances and times, film stars use vanity vans for various jobs such as commuting from one location to another, as living space, workstation, entertainment system, bedroom, gymnasium, and restroom.

2. **Jobs-to-b-done innovation must solve problems with poor solutions or no solutions**

   We can understand that jobs-to-be-done innovation should solve a problem with no solution. Sometimes customers have solutions to their problems, but those solutions are not adequate. For example, having own car and commuting with it has many problems such as it being expensive because of its purchase price and running and maintenance costs, people do not want to drive in heavy traffic, and there are parking problems. The available solution was taxies. People can commute in taxis, but it was expensive and difficult to find at every location. OLA taxis running on CNG solved these problems because they are affordable, and customers can book them through the OLA app. OLA taxis can come to customers' doorsteps within a few minutes, and customers can pay the fare through the OLA app.

3. **Other than functions, jobs have social and emotional dimensions**

   Products and services are surely meant to perform certain functions for customers, but jobs-to-be-done innovation is not just restricted to functions. It wraps the product or service with some actions that satisfy the customers' social and emotional needs. For example, Ritz-Carlton has become the world's leading brand in luxury hotels by setting its extraordinary service standards. One of its unbelievable policies is to permit every employee to spend up to $2,000 to make any single guest satisfied without seeking permission from the general manager. This $ 2000 limit is not for a year; rather, it is per incidence. If a waiter, for example, comes to know that today is his guest's birthday, he can serve a champagne bottle and some snacks as a gift in the guest's room for the birthday celebration. The idea is to do something to make a delightful stay for a guest and provide a wonderful experience to him that he can remember for a long time, and to satisfy the guest's social and emotional needs.

Case Study: Jobs-To-Be-Done Strategies of WhatsApp Business API

WhatsApp has quickly emerged as the go-to messaging app for over 1.6 billion consumers around the globe. It's a fast, simple, and convenient way for family and friends to chat, create group texts, share photos and videos, send and receive documents, and engage in private and secure conversations anytime, day or night.

To provide a secure, scalable solution to medium and large businesses, Facebook introduced the WhatsApp Business API in August 2018. This application programming interface (API) allows businesses to receive and answer unlimited WhatsApp messages from their customers. It was launched to help companies that wanted to use WhatsApp to communicate with multiple customers at scale. WhatsApp Business API enables businesses to automate communications with automated replies, and WhatsApp chatbots & interactive messages. In short, WhatsApp Business API helps businesses to create a personalized communication flow that works best for their customers.

WhatsApp Business API has adopted Jobs-To-Be-Done strategies to compete with email and other messaging channels like SMS, MMS, RCS, and LINE, which are long been the most common channels that businesses are using to connect with their customers.

Today, WhatsApp Business API messaging services have become a game-changer strategy for many business organizations. WhatsApp Business API services are performing the following five major jobs for their clients.

1. **Connecting Company's Brand with Customers**
   WhatsApp provides a secure and personal environment to customers by verifying all business accounts. Companies can communicate one-on-one with their customers. Using WhatsApp, companies create fully branded business identities, which allows them to provide email and phone contacts, social media links, office, and store addresses, website URLs, business details, and offers. Since WhatsApp facilitate multimedia communications, hence various brands can move beyond simple text or email and can communicate their brand character in uniquely new ways to make even more engaging customer connections.

2. **Connecting with Customers Anytime Anywhere in the World**
   Traditional communication channels such as the postal service, facsimile transmission, or telephonic conversation, and even digital communication channels like email or SMS, are no longer meeting the customer's demand because customers are viewing these channels at a fixed time. But WhatsApp is always open on their mobiles, and they are viewing it several times a day. Companies are now providing the ultimate customer experience by using WhatsApp messaging services. Dimensions Data Survey has revealed that nine out of ten consumers prefer using messaging to communicate with business organizations. Embracing WhatsApp, SnapTravel has expanded globally and provides more freedom to customers to reach SnapTravel and find and book hotel rooms on whatever messaging channels they prefer. Nielsen's survey discloses that 56% of the customers are preferring to message customer service than to speak on the phone.

3. **Global Spread**

   Except for China where people tend to prefer WeChat for business communications, WhatsApp is the number one messaging app in Latin America, Europe, Africa, and Asia. It has up to 95% smartphone penetration in many localities. Now almost all business houses worldwide are using WhatsApp for their customer care department and linking their customers through WhatsApp.

4. **Instant Two-Way Communications**

   Today, customers want two-way real conversations with businesses and not just receiving one-way messages from them. Earlier through other channels, two-way instant communications had certain issues such as regulatory restrictions, poor phone connectivity, a large workforce requirement to connect with a large number of customers through phone at any point in time, and unavailability of customers on phones due to their busy schedules. WhatsApp has resolved these issues and provides a flexible platform for instant two-way one-to-one secure conversations through text messages, voice & video chat, pictures, and videos.

5. **Private and Secure Conversations**

   End-to-end encryption and subscriber privacy protection is WhatsApp's most significant benefit, which businesses and customers are availing of. One of the most significant benefits of WhatsApp is its end-to-end encryption and strict attention to protecting subscribers' privacy. Today almost all top HR firms are using WhatsApp for conducting confidential interviews and exchanging texts, videos, and documents.

Chapter 5

Strategic Implementation

5.1 Activities Under Strategic Implementation

The third stage of strategic management, after strategic analysis and choice, is strategic implementation. It is also called strategic execution. At this stage, real action takes place in the strategic management process, and the strategic choice is transmuted into actual performance. What and why questions of the initial two stages are being answered in this by implementing how will we do it, who will do it, when will it be done, and where will it be done? Participation from the entire organization is required for strategic implementation.

The key strategic activities necessary for the effective execution of strategy include resource allocation, restructuring, business process reengineering, staffing, and training of employees, building a motivational climate, and developing high-performance culture.

5.2 Resource Allocation

Resource Allocation plays a significant role in the organization, and the managers must be aware of the capabilities and availability of resources. Resource allocation is assigning and managing tangible assets to support employees to achieve the organization's strategy. For example, if you want to reduce the production cost using automation, you need to allocate money to buy machines, computers, and software.

Proper resource allocation helps greatly in finishing the tasks without compromising the quality. This, in turn, improves overall business productivity. For effective resource allocation, we should be critically aware of the organization's objectives, strategy, available resources, and various activities that are to be performed.

1. **Steps involved in the resource allocation process**
- **Divide the Strategic Goals into Various Tasks:** This step clarifies how to achieve the strategic goals by accomplishing smaller tasks and what and how much resources are required to accomplish the tasks with desired quality standards.
- **Allocate the Resources to Each Task:** Allocate appropriate and adequate resources (Men, Machines, Materials, and Money) required to perform the activity. The resources should not be allocated excessively for one task or redundantly in different tasks. Judicial allocation of resources to various tasks eliminates redundant and excessive resource allocation, reducing the wastage of resources such as money, labor hours, machine hours, and raw materials.
- **Monitor Proper Utilization of Resources:** The final step in resource allocation is monitoring and ensuring the proper utilization of resources. A manager must ensure that activity should not underutilize or overutilize the resources.

5.3 Restructuring Organizational Structure

Almost every company uses an organizational structure to perform its business operations. Under the organizational structure, the different departments and positions are organized at different levels (Mainly top, middle, and front levels).

Organizational structures are normally demonstrated in the form of a chart like a pyramid, where the members having the responsibility for the whole organization are placed at the top level. In contrast, those having functional responsibility and authority related to their job domain are placed at the bottom. These major levels are also subdivided into sublevels. The organizational structure determines who is reporting to whom, who does what, and how the responsibility, authority, information, and decision-making is flowing between the departments and levels. For example, in a centralized structure, decision-making power is concentrated at the top level. In contrast, in a decentralized structure, decision-making power is distributed at various levels in the organization. A successful organizational structure defines each department and position's roles, responsibilities, authority, and how it fits within the overall system.

Sometimes key changes in the organizational structure are needed to achieve the chosen strategy. These changes include creating new departments or abolishing some of the existing departments, eliminating a few levels in the organizational hierarchies, reducing or expanding the span of control, creating new positions in the organizational structure, and changing roles, responsibilities, and authorities of various positions, and finally linking and relinking various departments.

Restructuring of Organizational Structure at Tesla

Tesla manufactures electric cars and was founded in 2003. Recently to penetrate the market deeper and increase its market share, Tesla made strategic goals such as reducing the overall cost of operations, improving the cash flow, and increasing the share price. To achieve these strategic goals, Tesla decided to make the organizational structure's pyramid flatter and develop a team-based structure. It removed some hierarchy lines of its pyramidal structure, mostly from the middle levels, and develop self-directed teams at a front level. Tesla laid off 3000 salaried employees to reduce redundancy and excessive staff. Now the front-level supervisors report directly to top-level managers, the communication from both ends has been improved. The authority to make strategic decisions is given to self-directed teams on the front line.

5.4 Business Process Reengineering

A business process is a collection of interrelated activities designed to accomplish the stated outcome. Business Process Reengineering (BPR) is an endeavor to redesign the core business processes to improve productivity, and product quality, and reduce the cost of operations. This requires analysis and redesigning of workflows, eliminating redundant work, inventory management, inbound and outbound logistics, making or buying decisions, and continuous improvement.

BPR involves eliminating redundant or unnecessary activities, adding new activities if required, and developing a more efficient and effective sequence of interrelated activities. Therefore, BPR entails developing a completely new business process replacing the existing one to achieve extraordinary improvements in productivity, cycle times, quality, cost reduction, and responsiveness toward customers. BPR is not a business process improvement (BPI), which is involved in improving the existing process, whereas BPR replaces the existing process with a new one.

1. **How to reengineer the business process?**
   There are four steps to re-engineer a business process illustrated hereunder:

- **Draw a flow diagram of the existing business process:** It's important to have a clear picture of an existing process regarding several activities, people, departments, and the sequence of activities. For getting a clear picture, the best way is to draw a flow diagram of an entire process on a piece of paper.
- **Identify various activities and departments involved:** Once a flow diagram of a process is ready, we can easily identify the number of activities and their sequence, and the number of departments involved in the process and performing different jobs. We should also identify new activities or departments that need to be added.
- **Incorporate Information Technology:** Today, almost all activities are using information technology to speed up the process through a quick and smooth flow of information both within and across the processes. For example, in the past, secretaries were typing the notices of the head of the institutions. Then, after the signature from the heads, the notices were pasted on the institutions' notice boards by the peon. But nowadays head of the institution is drafting the notices by himself and sending them to all the employees through WhatsApp, emails, or uploading the notices on the institution's website.
- **Redesign and implement the process:** Once the previous steps have been followed properly, it is time to develop new alternatives in the form of a flow diagram. While redesigning the process, we must ensure that all the desired activities are correct to eliminate the wastage of resources. In addition, we must use relevant equipment and IT services to ensure an efficient and rapid flow of information. Finally, after developing a few alternatives, we should select and implement the process which is best suited to the organization's strategy.

Reengineering of Purchase and Payable Process at Ford Motors

Ford motors identified excess staff in their accounts department, almost two times more than competitors of the same size.

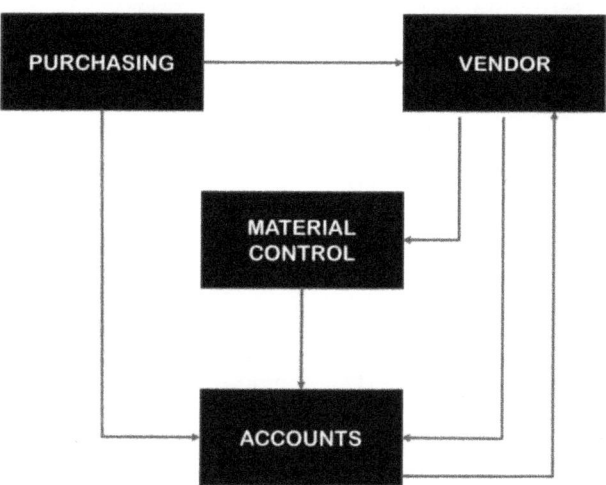

Figure 5.1: Purchasing and Payable Process

Under a low-cost strategy, Ford Motors decided to reduce the number of employees to half in its accounts department. As shown in figure 5.1., the process designers draw a flow diagram of Ford's purchasing and payable process to know the optimal number of employees required to perform the entire process. They found the following departments and activities in the process:

- Purchasing department prepares and gives the purchase order to the vendor and sends a copy of the same to the accounts department.
- Vendors supply the material and supply documents to the material control department and send a copy of the invoice to the accounts department.

- The accounts department collects the material receipt document from the material control department and matches it with the purchase order and invoice sent by the vendor.
- Finally, if everything is found correct accounts department releases the payment to the vendor.

As shown in figure 5.2 below, while reengineering the existing process, designers decided to create a centralized database that can be accessed by the purchase, material control, and accounts departments. Following are the flow of activities of the re-engineered purchasing and payable process:

- The purchase department issues a purchase order to the vendor and updates the centralized database.
- A vendor sends the goods to the material department along with supply documents and invoices.
- The material department cross-checks the supply document and invoice with the purchase order stored on the centralized database and updates the information regarding the receipt of goods and invoices on the database.
- The accounts department releases the payment according to the invoice stored in the database by the material control department and updates the payment information in the database.

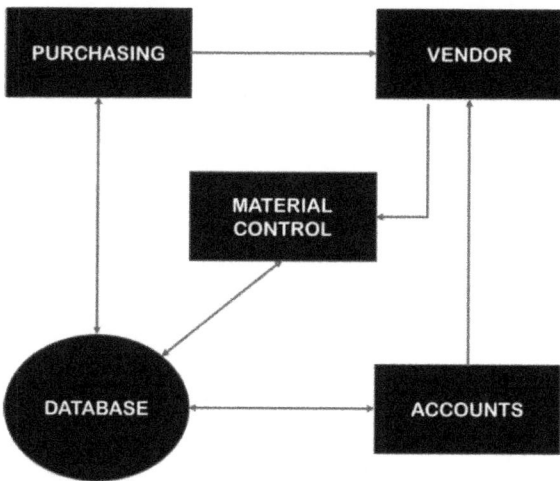

Figure 5.2: Reengineered Purchasing and Payable Process

5.5 Staffing

At the strategic execution stage, we must answer two questions: "Do we have an adequate number of employees to implement the strategy?" and "Do we have skilled employees in the organization to implement the strategy?"

The first concern about an adequate number of employees is easier to address because we can hire additional manpower. The second concern is difficult, as we need to ensure that the existing employees have the necessary skills, knowledge, and competencies required to perform various tasks to achieve strategic goals. If the current employees lack the required skills and competencies, they should be given the necessary training and workshops to develop them to put the strategic plan into action.

Staffing is the process of hiring eligible candidates for specific positions and providing them necessary training to develop the required skills, knowledge, and competencies to achieve strategic goals. Staffing is one of the most important management functions because it fills the vacant positions with the right personnel in the right job at the right time. The following steps are required:

1. **Identify Requirements**

   The recruiter must identify the vacant positions in the organization needed to put a strategy into action. At the same time, it is imperative to create new specific positions matching strategy requirements.

2. **Develop Job Descriptions**

   For hiring the right people for various vacant or created positions, writing each position's job description is important. A job description is a document that clearly states various job duties, responsibilities, skills, and knowledge needed to perform the job at a specific position. Writing a complete job description guides the recruiter to find and select candidates that are a good fit for the role. It also helps hold the candidate accountable if they are not performing their duties as per the job description. In addition, clear job descriptions posted on job posting sites attract the right candidates who are a good fit for the position. An effective job description contains the job title, job overview, job responsibilities and duties, required skills, competencies, knowledge, education, and experience. A sample of a job description is compiled in table 5.1 below.

	Sample Job Description of Sales Representative
Job Title	Sales Representative
Reports to:	Sales Manager
Job Overview	We are looking for Sales Representatives who can ensure that our current customers have the right products and services, identify prospective buyers, convert them into our customers, and maintain relations with them.
Responsibilities & Duties	<ul><li>Serves customers by selling products and meeting their needs.</li><li>Serve existing customers, obtains orders, and establish new accounts by planning and organizing a daily work schedule to call on existing or potential sales outlets and other trade factors.</li><li>Monitor competition by gathering current marketplace information on pricing, products, new products, delivery schedules, and merchandising techniques.</li></ul>
Skills, Competencies, and Knowledge	<ul><li>Meeting Sales Goals</li><li>Territory Management</li><li>Prospecting skills</li><li>Negotiation Skills</li><li>Presentation Skills</li><li>Closing skills</li><li>Product knowledge</li><li>Industry Knowledge</li><li>Maintaining Relationships with Customers</li></ul>
Educational Qualification and Experience	<ul><li>MBA degree with a specialization in Marketing from a recognized University.</li><li>Three to five years of industry sales experience</li><li>Familiarity with Microsoft Office software and phone systems</li></ul>

Table 5.1: Sample of Job Description of a Sales Representative

3. **Recruitment**

The objective of recruitment is to attract an adequate number of potential candidates having the necessary skills, knowledge, qualifications, and experience for the positions in the organization. Therefore, recruitment can be defined as searching for potential employees and appealing to them to apply for the positions available in the organization. There are various activities involved in the recruitment of process, which are elucidated hereunder:

- **Identification of various sources for manpower supply:** There are two main sources of manpower supply viz., internal, and external sources. Utilizing internal sources, a company can find suitable candidates from its existing employees working in different departments. Then, the selected employees get transferred from their units to the vacant position or promoted to the same department to fill the vacant position. For example, a salesperson can be transferred to the product management department with or without promotion, otherwise, an employee working in the product management department can be promoted to fill the position.

  A company can post job ads in daily newspapers, magazines, job websites such as timesjob.com, company's website, job ads on radio and TV channels, listing requirements in government employment exchange, hiring through private employment agencies, or directly hiring through campus placements.

- **Validation and selection of various external sources:** Posting ads on external recruitment sources requires money investment. Therefore, it is essential to assess various sources regarding their brand, reach, circulation, and credibility among prospective candidates. In the case of newspapers and magazines, the company wants to know about their circulation and the class of readers. On a job-search website number of clicks or the size of

the traffic indicates the reach of the sites to prospective candidates. The company checks the institutions' recognition and affiliations, infrastructure, admission process, and teaching standards to select educational institutions for a campus recruitment drive.
- **Inviting Applications:** Finally, after selecting external recruitment sources, the company invites applications from prospective candidates.

4. **Selection of Candidates**

After collecting an adequate number of applications from prospective candidates, the process of selection starts. Selection is choosing the appropriate candidates from the pool of collected applications through various screening methods. The various types of screenings and their proper sequence are mentioned hereunder:

- **Preliminary Screening**: In the preliminary screening process, the review of candidates' biodata is done to select all the probable candidates. For the screening, the focus is on candidates' educational qualifications, experience, and age.
- **Online Written Test:** Today majority of companies are conducting online written tests to know about candidates' aptitudes, attitudes, personality traits, and interests.
- **Group Discussion:** After selecting the most potential candidates from the written test, group discussions are in a group of 10 candidates are conducted to know the candidates' oratory, expressions, team spirit, and leadership qualities.
- **Personal Interview:** The personal interview of high potential candidates is conducted to know their job attitude, ability to face tough situations, persistence, and subject knowledge. Finally, the most suited candidates are selected.

- **Reference Checks:** Reference cross-checks and background cross-checks of all the selected candidates are done from their previous organizations and the references given by the candidates.
- **Medical Examination:** Candidates' medical examination reports are important to ensure that they are physically and mentally fit to perform the job and not carry any infectious disease.
  o **Job Offer:** Finally, the company issues appointment letters to all the selected candidates.

5. **Training & Development:** Training and development is an effort to improve employees' performance by developing their skills, competencies, knowledge, and attitude.

   Training: Training increases employees' ability, skills, and knowledge to perform the job. There are two broad platforms such as on-the-job and off-the-job, on which the training is given to employees. The training methods used at the on-the-job platforms are apprenticeship programs, job rotation, internship training, and mentorship. The methods used at off-the-job platforms are classroom lectures, online lectures, videos, vestibule training, role-plays, etc.

   - **Apprenticeship Programs:** Apprenticeship is a combination of on-the-job training and academic guidelines. Apprenticeship is not an internship as the internship is purely on-the-job training of students. Apprenticeship programs are designed for full-time employees in which the participants first take the academic lectures in the classroom and then immediately after they apply the lessons through working.
   - **Job Rotation:** Job rotation is a routine of lateral shifting of employees to different jobs at the same level in an organization. For example, an employee working loan department is shifted to

the teller counter for a specified period in the banks. Employees come to their original job after completing an entire rotation cycle. The objectives behind the practice of job rotation are to provide employees with opportunities to learn new skills required to perform different jobs and get exposure to new roles and responsibilities. In addition, it is an excellent way to give on-the-job cross-training to employees. Working at one job may range from one week to six months, depending on the company's job rotation program.

- **Mentorship:** On-the-job mentoring is a system of semi-structured guidance from senior employees (mentors) to junior employees (mentees) to share knowledge, skills, and experience. It is the authoritative and nurturing relationship between a more experienced person and a less experienced person. It is the best way to clone corporate knowledge. It helps employees to reach their full personal and professional potential. Mentoring provides the best way to customize the development of careers to serve the corporation's mission and helps in developing corporate culture. It helps greatly generate employees' commitment to organizational values and develop high-performance organizational culture, competencies, and core competencies. Mentors in the organization help their mentees grow in their career path by building trustful relationships with them, identifying their hidden potential, and nurturing their potential to grow in their career path and life. Mentors align their mentees with the organization's vision and strategic goals, mutually set their personal goals, help them to develop action plans to achieve the goals, and finally inspire them and provide emotional support.

- **Classroom/Online Lectures:** Off-the-job training is done in the classroom where a trainer imparts the knowledge to trainees. Nowadays, classroom teaching is shifting to online mode, and employees can join online classes or videos by being at their homes and without disrupting their office hours.

- **Vestibule Training:** Under vestibule training, new employees learn to use machines or equipment, but the training is conducted away from the actual job floor. For example, air pilots are given training in the simulated cockpit. Thus, vestibule training is also called near-the-job training.

Development: Development refers to creating certain development programs and opportunities to help employees grow both in their skills and knowledge and in their careers and life. Today, many companies are embracing responsibilities to develop their employees' careers and life satisfaction. Training is given to enable the employees to perform their jobs better, whereas development programs are conducted to enable the overall growth of the employees. Thus, development is a career-oriented process.

5.6 Building Leadership at All Levels

Building effective leadership at all levels of the organization is exceptionally important to align all the resources with the strategic objectives and generate extraordinary organizational performance.

The traditional approach to leadership is characterized by a top-down philosophy, where the leaders are decisive, efficient, unemotional, and in total control. On the other hand, the post-industrial paradigm is characterized by networks of mind, power-sharing facilitation, and empowerment. The best leaders do not want to be applauded by people. Their physical presence merely exists, but their aroma is always present in the organizational climate. In today's organizations, leaders operate in a shared-powered environment with followers. A single leader does not have all the answers and the power to make substantial changes in the organization. They need support from their empowered people.

If you are regularly involved in planning, organizing, controlling, and managing all the operations efficiently, you are doing excellent managership but certainly **NO** leadership at all. Many managers think they are doing great leadership because they monitor day-to-day operations, manage the resources, involve people with the already taken initiatives by the management, and be involved in the processes of lean management, benchmarking, cost management, inventory management, or supply chain rationalization. But do believe that these are not leadership. According to Peter Drucker, leadership is not making friends and influencing people to work, i.e., salesmanship. What is leadership, then?

Leadership is the lifting of man's vision to higher sights, raising man's personality beyond its normal limitations. This can only be done through Nurturing Leadership. Leadership is involved in providing the right direction to people and getting them to do what they do not want to and like that too. Leaders are altruistic. If you are a leader, you lose the right to think about yourself. If you think you are indispensable, you are not a leader because leaders are consistently involved in transforming their followers into great leaders. Leaders are not offering jobs to people; instead, great leaders provide signature experience to their subordinates.

Employees get signature experience when they get ample opportunity to perform, proper mentoring to grow personally and professionally, the opportunity to become the best expression of themselves, and achieve extraordinary heights in their career. They get signature experience when they feel happy, joyful, filled with positive energy, and working in a high-performance culture with wonderful people around. To generate signature experience in the organization, leaders relentlessly perform certain leadership functions such as envisioning, aligning, mentoring, motivating, empowering, and building a high-performance culture. We can appreciate leadership better if we clearly understand the distinction between leadership and managerial approaches.

1. **Leadership Vs. Management**

    The irony of today's organizational scenario is that despite having tremendous knowledge of leadership, there is a crisis of practicing leaders in organizations. According to John Kotter, today, organizations are overly managed and underled. There are two alternate reasons behind overly managed organizations. Firstly, managers at various levels are not acquainted with the differences between leadership and managerial approaches and consider their managerial practices as leadership practices. Secondly, perhaps they are so engrossed and busy in their routine managerial functions that they do not get time to practice leadership roles. According to current thinking, leadership deals with change, inspiration, motivation, and influence. In contrast, management deals more with maintaining equilibrium and the status quo. Managers concentrate on the bottom line to stabilize systems within the paradigm, whereas leaders investigate the horizons to bring the required changes in the organization. Thus, leaders work between the paradigms. We can manage materials but cannot manage human beings as they have their thoughts and emotions. They can be led only. Therefore, leaders concentrate on guiding or leading people toward the right destination.

2. **Summary of Leadership Vs. Management**

   On one end, both the leadership and managerial practices are completely different; on the other end, these two practices are complementary to each other. Leadership is not the replacement of management functions. One cannot get success by just practicing one approach. Equal weightage must be given to both leadership and managerial approaches. According to Steven Covey, leadership makes sure that the ladders we are climbing are leaning against the right wall, and management makes sure that we are climbing the ladder in the most efficient ways possible. Leadership begins where management ends, where systems of rewards, punishment & controls give way to innovation, empowerment, individual character, and the courage of convictions. Once the companies understand the fundamental differences between leadership and management, they groom their managers to provide both. The managers work within the paradigm, eliminate the risks, and stabilize the system, whereas leaders work between the paradigms, take risks, and disrupt the system. Managers administer and create order in the system, but the leaders innovate and develop new practices. Through appropriate planning, organizing, and controlling, managers keep an eye on the bottom-line performances of the organization. Whereas through envisioning, aligning, and empowerment, leaders keep an eye on the horizon.

5.7 Functions of Leadership

Although I am describing leadership functions at this strategic implementation stage, these functions are all-pervasive. Therefore, they must be consistently performed in all the stages of the strategic management process from the beginning.

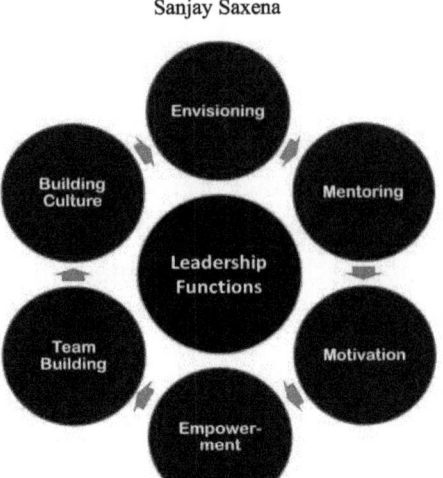

Figure 5.3: Functions of Leadership

1. Envisioning

Envisioning is the process of creating a distant picture in mind, developing strategies to achieve created picture, and taking actions to convert the vision into a real physical entity. Envisioning is the first step of the organizational leadership process. Any attempt to perform a leadership role without a vision is destined to fail. An important part of your job as a leader is to set a course toward the future and get everyone in the organization moving in the same direction. Employee motivation and energy are crucial to the success of all organizations; the role of leadership is to focus everyone's energy on the same path. Many so-called managers in the corporate world feel that leadership is all about developing friendships with subordinates and influencing them to do the job. Real leaders lift the vision of their employees and take them to a destination, which they have never thought of. One study found that, on average, senior executives in today's organizations spend less than 3 percent of their time and energy on building a corporate perspective for the future. In some companies, the average is less than 1 percent. As a leader, you need to detach yourself from bottom line working or from the trap of daily routine and investigate the horizons to set the right direction for the organization and align all the stakeholders with it.

2. Building Motivational Climate

Motivation is derived from the word "motive." Motive means drives, needs, or desires within the individual. Individual, showing willingness and putting effort to achieve certain things to satisfy his need or desire is motivation. A leader's job is to induce this willingness among employees to put effort into achieving their organization and personal goals. It is a set of processes that determine behavioral choices. Motivation is the vital link between knowing and doing, thinking and action, and competence and performance. According to classical need-based theories, motivation results from the interaction of a person's needs and external influences that determine behavior designed to achieve a goal. Before we understand how leaders motivate their people, we need to understand the types of basic human needs, which are one of the important sources of motivation.

Maslow's Hierarchy of Needs

As shown in figure 5.4., Abraham Maslow hypothesized that within every human being there exists a hierarchy of five need categories. He arranged all five need categories in priority order of importance. Priority goes above from the most basic needs (Physiological) to the most complex (Self-Actualization) needs.

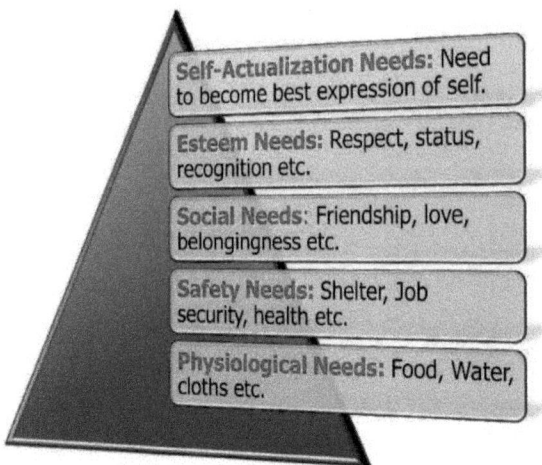

Figure 5.4: Maslow's Hierarchy of Needs

A person moves to the next level of the need category when the present level of the need category is minimally satisfied. Leaders are utilizing this theory for better job design, compensation, reward planning, developing training programs, and framing organizational policies and practices to satisfy employees' needs.

- **Physiological Needs**

  These are basic bodily needs of people like food, water, sex, and clothes. Leaders try to satisfy these needs with adequate salaries, promotion to higher paying positions, financial incentives and rewards, gift schemes, various types of allowances, and other benefits.

- **Safety Needs**

  Need for shelter, job security, life security, and health safety are prominent in this category. To satisfy these needs leader works on job security, retirement benefits, pension plans, clean and hygienic workplace, life and health insurance, and emergency medical facilities in the work premises.

- **Social Needs**
  Need for affiliation, friendship, love, affection, social acceptance, and belongingness. To satisfy the above-stated needs, leaders create opportunities for productive social gatherings through conferences, workshops, presentations, annual meet, and regular celebrations for successful goal accomplishments. Today, companies are sponsoring their productive employees to get memberships in social clubs, country clubs, and sports clubs.
- **Esteem Needs**
  Esteem needs are like the need for respect, social status, recognition, higher self-esteem, etc. Leaders give recognition and achievement certificates at the annual meets of the organization, publish success stories in the company's newsletter, write appreciation letters to achievers, and ask people to give achievers a warm round of applause during goal achievement celebrations.
- **Self-Actualization Needs**
  People under this need category want to become the best expression of themselves. They want to utilize their potential fully. Their self-actualization need gets satisfied when they generate extraordinary performance, learn new skills, develop competencies, and acquire great knowledge. They want to be highly creative and express themselves in a great manner. To satisfy their self-actualization needs, leaders help them chart their careers, provide opportunities to learn new skills and develop competencies in their passionate area, and send them abroad for training and education.

Extrinsic & Intrinsic Motivation

With extrinsic motivation, we do things because the outcomes of the activities will bring about situations that we like, or which allow us to avoid unpleasant events. For example, sometimes we work to earn money to pay for food, accommodation, and entertainment or we work hard to complete tasks so that we can avoid losing our job.

With intrinsic motivation, we do things because we start enjoying the activities themselves. For example, we sing a song in isolation because we enjoy singing. Intrinsic motivation is generated during the process and is self-rewarding. In many research outcomes, intrinsically motivated people have shown more confidence, interest, involvement, and excitement in the task. Self-determination theory was developed by professors Richard Ryan and Edward Deci to explain conditions that foster intrinsic motivation. Within this theory, intrinsic motivation is conceptualized as the inclination we have towards spontaneous interest, exploration, and mastery of new information, skills, and experience. People show higher persistence, self-esteem, and subjective well-being when they are intrinsically motivated. Subjective well-being occurs when a person is full of positive emotions. The self-determination theory predicts that when our needs for competence, relatedness, and autonomy are satisfied, intrinsic motivation is likely to occur, but it will be less likely when these needs are not satisfied. Strong belief in our skills and competencies leads to our initiation for challenging tasks because we feel that we can do these tasks successfully. It gives us personal satisfaction. For motivating people, leaders design the jobs and frame the policies in such a way that needs for competence, relatedness, and autonomy should be fulfilled.

Csikszentmihalyi's Concept of Flow Experience

Our intrinsic motivation reached its peak in the form of a flow experience. Flow experience occurs when we become completely engrossed in controllable but challenging tasks or activities. We become so much involved in the task that we forget our worries and frustrations, and our time perception gets altered, which means we feel that hours are passing in minutes. Our sense of self disappears during our flow experience and surprisingly the sense of self reappears as a more strengthened self after the task is completed. Flow experience commonly occurs when we are watching movies or sports, playing games, reading books, listening, or playing music, and giving board exams, etc. The following conditions are important for the flow experience to occur:

- **Challenging yet Achievable Task:** The task must be challenging yet achievable.
- **Perceived Importance of Task:** The perceived task's importance must be high, which means the task should be especially important for the person who is doing it.
- **Utilizing different types of Skills to complete the task:** When a person is using a variety of skills for completing the task, flow experience is likely to occur.
- **Autonomy for Making Choices:** Leaders must provide autonomy in making choices and immediate feedback to people doing the task.

The lack of challenge and skill variety required to accomplish the task, tough management controls, overbearing structures, and hierarchies, create barriers to flow experience.

What happens when leaders try to motivate people who are not interested?

When followers are not interested or frustrated due to poor organizational climate or poor relationships with supervisors, then anything you say is just a kick for them. Let us see the types of kicks that leaders are unsuccessfully using on their pupils for generating motivation:

- **Positive Kick**

  Leaders give positive counseling to followers by making them aware of the positive consequences of their positive actions, but subordinates who are frustrated with the system, reject the leader's words and think that nothing is going to improve here. In this case when you are trying to provide positive counseling to your frustrated subordinates, who are motivated, you or your pupils?

- **Negative Kick**

  When you are failed to convince your people through positive counseling you adopt another way and start giving negative counseling to them by making them aware of the negative consequences of their negative actions. Still, the result is the same in your followers. They listen to you from one ear and remove everything from another ear. In putting your efforts to motivate your frustrated people, who is motivated, you or your follower?

- **Real Kick**

  When nothing works then you feel that now the time has come, and you should implement things the hard way. You give some kinds of punishment like an explanation call, salary deduction, suspension, etc., to your pupils to bring them on track. People consider these punishments as real kicks. Here again who is motivated you or your people?

- **Return Kick**
  In reaction to a real kick, followers give a return kick to you, like resignation, court case, violence, etc.

Building Motivational Climate Using Herzberg Two Factor Motivation Theory

The phenomena narrated above are a regular feature in many organizations. The solution to the above problem was given by Frederick Herzberg. In his opinion, building a motivational climate in the organization is imperative to generate work satisfaction among employees. Once a motivational climate is developed then all other efforts to motivate employees will give positive results. For this purpose, Herzberg depicted the two-factor theory of motivation, in which he identified different motivating factors falling into two categories i.e., Hygiene Factors and Growth Factors. These two categories of factors are responsible for the satisfaction and dissatisfaction of employees. Further, as shown in table 5.2, Herzberg recognized that the opposite of satisfaction is not dissatisfaction, rather, it is no satisfaction. In the same way, the opposite of dissatisfaction is not satisfaction, rather, it is no dissatisfaction. Therefore, the continuum of satisfaction moves from dissatisfaction to no dissatisfaction and finally from no dissatisfaction to satisfaction.

Dissatisfaction ----- No-Dissatisfaction ----- Satisfaction	
Hygiene Factors	**Growth Factors**
• Company Policies	• Personal Growth
• Salary and Benefits	• Professional Growth
• Quality Supervision	• Recognition & Rewards
• Relationship with Peers	• Job Design
• Physical Environment	• Empowerment
• Social Status	• Sense of Ownership
• Job Security	• High-Performance Culture

Figure 5.2: Herzberg Two Factor Theory of Motivation

In the organization, when Hygiene factors are satisfied, then employees reach a no-dissatisfaction zone where they are neither satisfied nor dissatisfied. To generate satisfaction, we need to work on Growth Factors. Working on growth factors alone will not produce the required results unless hygiene factors are available in the organizational climate and employees are already in a no-dissatisfaction state of mind. As shown in Table 5.2., by establishing hygiene factors like employee-friendly policies, quality supervision, adequate salary, job security, and social status of employees, leaders can satisfy the physiological, security, and social needs of employees. Once these needs are satisfied, employees come into a state of no dissatisfaction. By establishing growth factors in the organizational climate such as personal growth, better job design, empowerment, and a sense of ownership, leaders can satisfy higher-order needs like esteem needs and self-actualization needs. They can generate intrinsic motivation and flow experience. For example, personal growth and professional growth factors directly satisfy people's self-actualization need to become the best expression of themselves. Performance recognition and & rewards can satisfy employees' esteem needs. Empowerment and better job design can generate intrinsic motivation and flow experience among employees.

Hygiene Factors

a. **Company's Policies:** Company policies are guidelines to help employers deal with administrative, health, safety, regulatory, legal, customer, and employee issues. Employee-friendly company policies increase employees' well-being. Although various policies help to smooth the functioning of the entire organization, some personal policies such as leave rules, no discrimination, health and insurance, work hours, vacation, and flexible-timing policies are exceptionally important for employee satisfaction. To enhance work-life balance for employees, the provision of casual leave, duty leave, medical leave, earned leave, study leaves, and childcare leave is crucial. Besides friendly leave policies, optimal working hours and flexible schedules are also important for enhancing work-life balance. To boost the employees' morale and sense of belongingness, the company should have a strict policy of no discrimination and equal opportunities for all employees. Employees' health and family interests must be protected by providing health and life insurance policies for each employee. Policy to maintain health hygiene at the workplace should be implemented meticulously.

b. **Salary and Benefits:** Salary is a fixed compensation paid at regular intervals (monthly or annually) to employees against their work in the form of money. Wages are paid hourly. How much salary can protect workers from dissatisfaction? Though there is no limit to the amount of salary paid to employees as per their qualifications and job profile, the salary should be compatible with industry standards at each level. Further, a good salary should fulfill the basic needs and lifestyles of employees and their families, and employees can save some amount of money for unwanted events and future security. Salaries must be augmented with some benefits. These benefits are health and life insurance, vacation pay, maternity leave, employer contribution in retirement benefits such as provident fund and pension, stock options, bonuses, etc.

c. **Quality Supervision:** Quality Supervision involves supporting and inspiring employees to perform their activities excellently and achieve extraordinary outcomes. Current research outcomes and supervisory practices suggest that effective supervisors are those who have the required managerial, leadership, and communication skills to provide support and guidance to their employees at the workplace. Supervisors should not micro-manage their subordinates; instead, they should provide autonomy, power, and emotional support. Quality supervisors establish productive relationships with people at the workplace, build strong teams, manage change, manage workflow, provide on-the-job training, evaluate performance, give feedback, resolve employees' issues and disputes, and provide mentoring support to their subordinates.

d. **Relationship with Peers:** Strong peer-to-peer relationships at the workplace increase employee engagement many folds. It reduces employee turnover and protects employees against job dissatisfaction. Mutual trust and respect, teamwork, a win-win attitude, and synergistic communication between employees are the key elements to strong peer relationships in the workplace. These connections could also serve as future references or contacts in employees' careers.

e. **Physical Environment:** The great physical environment in a workplace augments the productivity of people. It lifts the psychological and physical energy of people and boosts their morale and spirit. Proper lighting, noise-free conditions, moderate room temperature, air purity with good odor, clean dust-free furniture and other physical objects, clean office floors, and washrooms in the workplace certainly improve workers' work concentration and productivity.

f. **Social Status:** People working in reputed organizations such as Google, Microsoft, or Apple get special attention and respect from society. Society perceives them as skillful, competent, knowledgeable, and successful people. Today all business organizations want to establish themselves as a great brand. It's not necessary that the employees of large business houses only will get social recognition. Small organizations' employees can also get social recognition if their organization is ethical, add value to society, and provide valuable products and services to consumers.

g. **Job Security:** All the hygiene factors narrated above may not generate the desired results unless high job security exists in the organization. Every employee wants job security and certainty in life. In a state of insecurity, it is hard for employees to give their best. Today employees worry that they can be replaced by new hires who are fresh graduates from the universities and can work at lower pay. They can be fired due to large-scale automation in companies where machines and robots are taking over human jobs. Managers need to communicate to employees that they are valued, safe, secure, and have a bright future. Mere positive communication will not produce the desired results, and there must be proper mentoring of employees to grow them as skilled, competent, knowledgeable, diligent, and valuable employees. Job insecurity and value addition cannot coexist in the organization. If someone adds value to the organization through his great performance, his job insecurity will automatically be irradicated.

Growth Factors

a. **Personal Growth:** Personal growth is measured by the level of achievement of life goals, personal potential, wisdom, and values. Organizations consistently conduct development programs for their employees to nurture their potential, personality, wisdom, and values. Personal growth brings maturity and success in life and leads to life satisfaction. Managers in their role as mentors play an important role in motivating their mentees to put consistent efforts to develop themselves. Mentors make employees realize the importance of continual self-development in achieving life goals and life satisfaction. Companies are regularly organizing various employee development programs in important areas such as personality development, communication skills, emotional intelligence, leadership skills, selling skills, life management skills, etc.

b. **Professional Growth:** Professional growth of the employees refers to acquiring new skills and work experience, achieving job targets, generating excellent job performance, and getting promotions to higher positions in the organizational hierarchy. To help employees in their professional growth, many companies are doing certain things such as promoting from within, merging organizational needs with personal needs, building cross-functional teams, and offering learning resources. Promoting from within is one of the best techniques to motivate employees to stay in the company, put effort into developing their skills, and generate excellent performance. According to one of the Gallup studies, almost one-third of employees quit their jobs due to a lack of career advancement or promotional opportunities available in the organization. Promoting from within enhances employee engagement and inspires employees to professional development. In addition, working in cross-functional teams provides an opportunity for employees to learn new skills and perform roles beyond their job description.

c. **Recognition and Rewards:** To appreciate and motivate employees, the company recognizes and rewards them for their exceptional performances. Appreciation is one of the prominent human needs that should never be ignored, as employees always want to be appreciated for their work. When their work is recognized and rewarded by the company, their job satisfaction rises limitlessly. The rewards are both in cash and non-cash forms. Cash rewards are given to high-performing employees in the form of salary hikes, additional pay, or incentives. Non-cash rewards are highly effective and given in various forms elucidated as hereunder:

- **Handwritten Notes:** The top boss, such as the CEO or director, write a personal handwritten appreciation note to employees for their exceptional performance.
- **Executive Offer a Cup of Coffee:** Top executives invite high-performing employees to their office for a cup of coffee and talk to them about the company and its business.
- **Free Leave Pass:** Company gives a certain number of free days off to employees to use as they like. They can go to exotic locations, read a book, play with their kids, or do as they want.
- **Love from Co-workers:** Co-workers write something they truly admire about an employee on a colorful sheet of paper, then frame that sheet along with a photograph of the employee.
- **Applaud with Standing Ovation:** High-performing employees are given a standing ovation by all the employees in the annual general meeting.

- **Wall of Fame:** Employees who have accomplished something truly extraordinary are elected for placing their photos along with the details of their accomplishments on a wall of fame built in a company's premises.

d. **Job Design:** A job is a set of task activities that engage an individual in an organization. Job design is a meticulous effort to arrange tasks, responsibilities, and authority into a unit of work to achieve certain goals. A well-designed job can enhance intrinsic motivation and flow experience of employees and produce remarkable performance. Conversely, poorly designed jobs result in monotony, job dissatisfaction, high employee turnover, and poor performance. There are two basic methods to redesign jobs, job enlargement, and job enrichment.

   o **Job enlargement** is the horizontal expansion of job activities. It involves adding various activities in the periphery of an existing job at the same level in the organization. Job enlargement helps employees get rid of monotony by allowing them to perform a wider range of tasks. It also helps employees to learn a variety of skills and earn higher wages. Learning a variety of skills leads to better career growth. For example, a teacher can be highly motivated when he is empowered to develop course content, deliver lectures, evaluate students, and submit final grades to the board of studies.

   o **Job enrichment** is a vertically upward expansion of job activities. It's a vertical loading of motivating activities on the existing job. The existing job can be enriched by adding a few more activities from the upper level to make the existing job more challenging, creative, exciting, and rewarding. In addition, job enrichment provides more decision-making autonomy and power to the jobholders. For example, Ritz Carlton Hotels permit every employee to spend up to $2,000 to make any single guest satisfied without seeking permission from the general manager.

3. Empowerment

Empowerment is the process of increasing the capacity of individuals or groups, delegating power to them for making choices, and transforming those choices into desired actions and outcomes. To empower your employees, you need to trust them and be ready to tolerate their imperfections. Empowered people are more involved in the work, take-on difficult tasks, and act confidently. They put more sincere efforts into completing the task efficiently and effectively. The most common understanding of managers about empowerment is simply to delegate authority to make choices and decisions or share power with front-line employees. But this much understanding is not enough for true empowerment, and to design an effective empowerment program, you need to understand what must be shared with your employees.

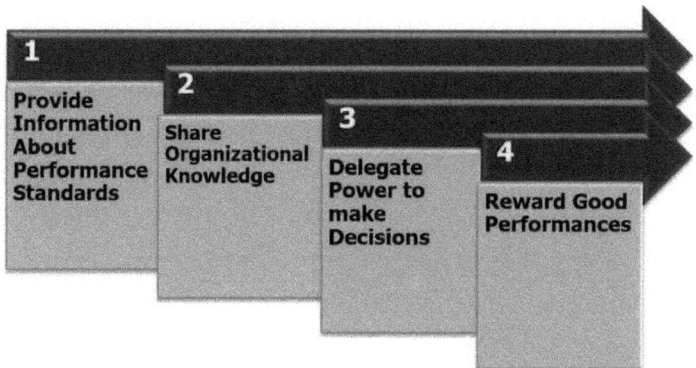

Figure 5.5: Bowen and Lawler Empowerment Model

As shown in figure 5.5., Bowen and Lawler (1995) defined empowerment as sharing four important organizational ingredients with front-line employees. First, the information about the organizational performance standards. The knowledge that enables employees to contribute effectively to organizational performance. Delegate power to make decisions that influence organizational direction and performance. Last but not least, excellent performances must be rewarded. Bowen and Lawler further added that even if one out of the four ingredients is missing, the empowerment would be zero.

Empowerment provides strong motivation because it meets the higher needs of individuals. Research indicates that individuals need self-efficacy, which is the individual's belief in his capacity to produce results or outcomes. Empowerment helps to remove the conditions that cause powerlessness while enhancing employees' feelings of self-efficacy. It also authorizes employees to cope with situations and enables them to control problems as they arise. Most people come into an organization with the desire to do a good job, and empowerment enables leaders to release the already existing motivation. Higher self-efficacy generates intrinsic motivation – a sense of personal mastery and competence. Empowerment increases the total amount of power in an organization.

Simply put, if everyone in the organization has power, then the organization is more powerful. The freedom from over-control allows subordinates to utilize their talents and abilities in ways that were otherwise constrained. Empowered employees use more of themselves to do their jobs. The leaders can devote more time to strategic issues as the empowered employees can handle day-to-day problems. Empowered subordinates bring innovations to the organization and can respond quicker and better to the markets they serve.

Why Empowerment Fails?

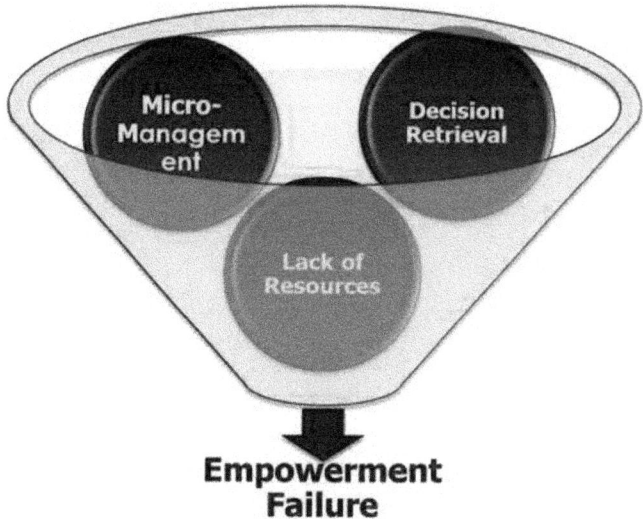

Figure 5.6: Reasons for Empowerment Failure

Other than the reason described above that empowerment will be zero if any of the four ingredients of the Bowen and Lawler empowerment model is missing, there are three more important reasons for empowerment failures, which are shown in figure 5.6.

- **Micromanagement:** Managers defined the decision-making authority and boundaries with staff, but then they micromanage employees' work. They need to know every action that employees are taking. They ask their employees to submit a daily report about everything that is happening on the ground. The employees get so much busy preparing the long reports that they forget their other important work. This is usually because managers do not trust their staff to make good decisions. One HR manager added ten days to the company's hiring process because he required his signature on every document in the process. The paperwork was buried on his desk for days, but the staff did not proceed without his signature. His lack of trust made employee empowerment a joke. Do employees make mistakes? Certainly, but fooling them about their boundaries is worse.

- **Lack of Resources:** Simply delegating the power to employees will not work. You need to provide them with all the necessary resources to work efficiently and effectively. For example, as an army officer at the border, you are empowered to make decisions during wartime. Still, your unit cannot survive long without backend supplies of ammunition, food, medical services, and technological support. In the same way, in a business organization, employees need necessary resources like machines, money, material, and advanced technology.

- **Decision Retrieval:** In the majority of organizations, empowerment fails because managers take back the delegated power from their employees. They are ready to make several mistakes by themselves, but they do not accept even a single mistake from their employees. For real empowerment, you need to tolerate your employees' imperfections. You can help staff make good decisions by coaching, training, and providing necessary information. You can even model good decision-making, but you must not change the empowerment decision unless a serious complication occurs. Teach the employee to make a better decision next time. But do not undermine their faith in their competencies and your trust, support, and admiration.

Sense of Ownership (Beyond Empowerment)

Today great leaders are moving beyond empowerment by generating a sense of ownership of the organization in their employees. Employees having a sense of ownership are working with a mindset of an owner. To generate this sense of ownership among employees, organizations allocate the company's stock to their employees. But these peanut stocks cannot generate a sense of ownership of the organization, and in many cases, employees sell their shares in the market when they get some profit. Sense of ownership is more psychological than financial. Let us examine what happens when employees work with workers' mindsets or vice versa.

Employees with workers' mindsets are worried about how their superiors perceive their actions. Therefore, they are inclined to protect their functional area and pursue their self-interests. They are persuaded to live by the rules, even if these rules are contrary to common sense. Rules are important to keep an organization's integrity, but common sense plays a vital role in some situations, and we need to make decisions against the rules even. Employees with a worker's mindset are concerned only about compensation, recognition, and rewards, which they are getting against their performance. They become satisfied if they perform well and receive appropriate rewards. Workers are happy to be controlled by their superiors and liked to be monitored. Workers are afraid to make risky decisions and initiatives because they know that they will have to give a written explanation upon failure.

Employees with an owner's mindset focus on the business results of their actions, regardless of who is watching. They bend, stretch, or even break the rule, which runs contrary to common sense. They are not afraid to make risky decisions and initiatives because they feel that it is their responsibility to grow the organization. They take initiative without being asked by superiors because they cannot be mere spectators. They understand that they are the ones who need to take action, nobody else will do it. They never think of leaving the organization even in their dreams because they see their workplace as the extension of their family. They consider the organization as their home, which they need to protect at any cost.

How to Engender Sense of Ownership?

For developing a sense of ownership among employees, the first step is to emotionally align them with the organizational vision. As a leader, you need to show complete trust in your employees' competencies and share organization-wide information with them. You should allow your employees to participate in strategic as well as organizational decision-making. Allow your employees to allocate the organizational resources by themselves only. You must tolerate the employees' imperfections and provide them the freedom to fail. Through proper mentoring, support your employees to overcome their limitations and imperfections. Implement a self-reporting system across the organization. Normally it is quite common practice in all organizations that employees report to their superiors regarding their initiatives, actions, performances, and issues. But in the self-reporting system, leaders encourage their employees to report to themselves only for their initiatives, actions, performances, and issues. The self-reporting system is based on the philosophy that owners are reporting to themselves only. Finally, you just discuss the results and ask them to find the solutions by themselves if there is any gap or issue.

4. Build Self-Directed Teams

Empowering employees as individuals or groups of individuals will not make much difference. You need to empower them in the form of self-directed teams. It is a reality of organizational life that one can rarely be successful alone, no matter how much they are empowered. Teams outperform individuals acting alone, especially when performance requires multiple skills, judgments, and experiences. Today in business organizations, self-directed teams are the mantra for success. According to Katzenbach and Smith (1993), "a team is a small number of people with complementary skills who are committed to a common purpose, common approach, and performance goals for which they hold themselves mutually accountable. In any situation requiring the real-time combination of multiple skills, experiences, and judgments, a team, without doubt, gives better results than a collection of empowered individuals operating within confined job roles and responsibilities. This mix of skills and experiences enables teams to respond to multifaceted challenges like innovation, quality, and customer service. Self-directed teams maximize the organization's human resources as each team member is coached, helped, and led by all the other team members. Success or failure is felt by all members, not just the individual. Failures are not blamed on individual members, which gives them the courage to take chances and initiative. Every team member feels successful, and this helps them to set and achieve bigger and better success. In addition, failure is perceived as a learning lesson.

Departments Vs. Self-Directed Teams

Traditionally the organizations' structures are divided into departments and sub-departments. For example, a business organization is broadly divided into the Marketing, Finance, Production, and Human Resource departments. The marketing department could be subdivided into advertising, distribution, or sales departments. In recently developed practices, leaders are dividing the entire organization into many self-directed teams and developing productive cooperation and coordination between self-directed teams. In a department, a group of people is not necessarily a team, and they may be a group of individuals for administrative convenience. A team is a group of people coming together to collaborate. This collaboration is to accomplish a shared goal for which they hold themselves mutually accountable. A team is a group of people with a high degree of interdependence geared towards the achievement of a common goal. Team members are deeply committed to each other's personal growth and success. This commitment usually transcends the team. A team outperforms a group and outperforms all reasonable expectations given to its members, i.e., a team has a synergistic effect...one plus one is equal to eleven or one hundred eleven, and not two.

Fundamentals of Self-Directed Teams

- **Small Number:** Large numbers of people have trouble interacting constructively as a team. A small number is more pragmatic to work productively with a common approach, complementary skills, and mutual accountability. The right size of a team should be 2 to 15 members. A larger number of people say fifty or more can theoretically become a team, but groups of such size will more likely break into sub-teams rather than function as a single team.
- **Shared Leadership Roles:** Successful team leaders instinctively know that the goal is the team's performance results instead of individual achievement, including their own. Team leaders believe that they do not have all the answers – so they do not insist on providing them. Therefore, the leadership roles are rotated according to different situations.
- **Team's Mission and Goals:** To convert a normal team into high performing self-directed team, leaders empower and facilitate team members to develop their team's mission and goals by themselves. Leaders make sure that each team member is participating actively in developing the team's mission and

goals. This exercise generates the team members' commitment to its mission and goals.

- **Consensus on Common Approach:** Once the team's mission and goals are agreed upon, it is time for team members to mutually develop a common approach to achieve the team's mission and goals. Team members must be agreed on who will do what, how schedules will be set and adhered to, the types of skills are to be developed, the conduct of each member of a team, the criteria and style of making decisions, and when and how to modify team's approach to get the job done. Agreeing on the specifics of work and how it fits together to integrate individual skills and development lies at the heart of generating commitment to a common approach.

- **Complementary Skills:** Common sense tells us that it is a mistake to ignore skills when selecting a team. A team cannot get started without some minimum complement of skills, especially technical and problem-solving ones. And no team can achieve its purpose without developing the multiple skills required. Therefore, the team should carry the right blend of complementary skills, that is, each of the complementary skills necessary to do the team's job. For example, in a marketing team of a product-based organization, there must be people with technical skills, selling skills, mass communication skills for advertising, logistics expert, IT experts, etc. On the other hand, suppose a team has only salespeople, then they may not be able to generate excellence where mass communication and IT skills are required. Thus, to generate excellence and achieve success, we should have the right mix of experts in different fields to complement each other.

- **Mutual Accountability:** No group ever becomes a team until it can hold itself accountable as a team. At its core, team accountability is about the sincere promises we make to ourselves and others for being accountable to the team's goals and performance results. For generating mutual accountability, trust is extremely significant. In addition, the members must be proactive in their habits as proactive persons understand their responsibility to take the initiatives to achieve the team's mission and goals and consider themselves accountable for consequences.

- **Excellent Performance Results:** In the final examination, the performance is both the cause and effect of teams. Other than specific and tangible performance results, everything else matters the least. Therefore, if you want to know whether any specific group is a real team, look first at its performance results.
- **Mutual Feedback:** Mutual feedback from team members is more authentic and transparent. It helps to develop feedforward for future performance, so that earlier mistakes could be rectified. It is not designed for giving rewards or punishments. It is purely to ensure better performance next time.
- **Equal Emotional Commitment with Each Other:** The high-performing self-directed teams differentiate themselves from normal teams based on the degree of emotional commitment, particularly how intensely the team members are emotionally committed to each other. Such commitments go much beyond common courtesies and teamwork. The team members' commitment to each other continues beyond even the life of the team itself. This commitment is not just the deep intimacy between team members; rather, it is everyone's strong personal commitment to one another's development, advancement, and success. Energized by this extra sense of interpersonal commitment, the team's purpose becomes more gracious to team members. People start considering one member's failure as their failure. The mutual concern for each other's development and success leads to the development of interchangeable skills

among team members and generates greater flexibility in the team. For example, in high-performance teams, the leadership role is rotated and shared with much more flexibility than in real teams. As a result, the team members carry a much better sense of contribution, humor, and fun.

5. Build Organizational Culture

In the past 40 years, the concept of organizational culture has gained wide acceptance to understand human systems. Increased competition in the era of globalization has created a greater need for organizational culture. Organizational culture can have a significant impact on the long-term financial performance of the organization. Organizational culture can enhance an organization's ability to take advantage of market opportunities or directly impede it. The culture of an organization influences the behavior of all employees; it guides their decision-making and governs the fundamental manner in which they go about their business. It is the hidden but unifying force that provides meaning and direction to the organization. It is learned, shared, and transferred from employee-to-employee overtime. It emerges naturally from people and systems. Organizational culture is possibly the most critical factor determining an organization's capacity, effectiveness, and longevity. It also contributes significantly to the organization's brand image and brand promise. Employees are much more likely to work for companies where they get signature experience, feel proud of, and where they enjoy a distinctive work environment. Culture serves three important functions in organizations:
1. It generates the signature experience and psychological energy needed to generate excellence.
2. It integrates members so that they know how to relate to one another.
3. It helps the organization adapts to the external environment.

6. Building Blocks of the Organizational Culture

Organizational culture is the personality of any organization. It is a common set of accepted organizational values, norms, and attitudes within the organization. These common sets of values, norms, and attitudes are reflected through visible phenomena of the organizational culture. These visible phenomena include stories, language, symbols, routines, rituals, and ceremonies. To build high-performance organizational culture, simply calling a meeting and telling employees about required behavior will not work. Instead, leaders must start from the building blocks of the organization.

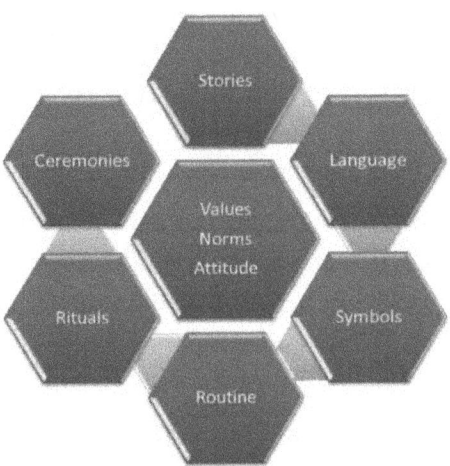

Figure 5.7: Building Blocks of the Organizational Culture

- **Widely Shared Organizational Values**

  The organization's values are the essential elements for every organization, which employees refer to in determining their behavior. The organizational values may be divided into two distinct yet highly related categories. These two categories are terminal values and instrumental values. The terminal value is the desired outcome that the organization wants to achieve. It includes such things as excellence, responsibility, profitability, innovativeness, equality, and customer satisfaction.

The instrumental value is the desired behavior of employees. It includes such things as communicating openly and honestly, being passionate and having fun, being helpful and supportive, taking the initiative and working hard, and being agile and flexible.

- **Widely Shared Norms**

  They influence the behavior of employees. Norms can be defined as a standard of interpersonal behavior of employees that the organization's members commonly accept. Norms are guidelines that prescribe appropriate behavior by employees in a specific situation. They are informal rules of behavior. They provide order to organizational activities

- **Widely Shared Attitude**

  In the organizational culture context, the attitude is not a positive or negative interpretation of the situation. Instead, it is the attitude in action to achieve organizational vision and goals. Examples of shared attitudes may be like:

  o Put a dent in a universe: We must do something extraordinary so that we can add exceptional value to people's life.

  o Jump the curve: We must create a new performance curve of extraordinary quality and revenue.

  o Work or does not work: Something may work or does not work, but we should not be afraid of adopting new approaches and jumping the curves.

  o Refuse to accept anything less than the best: We are not ordinary people. We are extraordinary, and we give our best and take the best.

- o Zero Tolerance: There should not be any compromise with discipline, excellent performance, and value-driven behavior.
- **Stories**

  The organization often shares success stories of its heroes, which illustrate the cultural values and norms of the organization. It provides good clues about the behavior expected in the organization. An organization with lots of success stories generates pride among the employees. They get the answers to the question of what it means to work here.
- **Language**

  Organizational language is an essential cultural element that allows employees to share their thoughts, feelings, and information in the organization. The words that employees use in their day-to-day conversations reveal the instrumental values of the organization. In addition, the formality in the language provides insight into the degree of hierarchy in the organizational structure, and the level of mutual respect that exists in the organization.
- **Symbols**

  Symbols serve as a visual representation of organizational values. Examples include dress codes, logos, office decors, furnishings, company vehicles, and hierarchical or horizontal organizational structures. These are non-verbal clues of shared organizational values by the members of the organization.
- **Routines**

  Routines are the everyday activities and behavior followed by the members of the organization. Routines can be observed by looking at what employees are doing everyday morning, daytime, and evening. How are they solving the problems and issues, and what procedure are they adopting to complete the tasks?

- **Rituals**
  Ritual is also a kind of routine, but it has special meaning, which brings the employees to gather for specific purposes at certain intervals. For example, employees attend the sales review meeting every month, board meetings are organized every quarter, etc.
- **Ceremonies**
  Many organizations arrange social events such as annual functions, picnics, birthday parties, etc., to demonstrate their cultural values and norms to employees and other stakeholders of the organization.

7. High-Performance Culture

There are many ways through which we can describe organizational culture, but for our convenience, we can define four different types of organizational cultures based on performance levels and employee-management relationships. Figure 5.8. given below shows four different types of organizational culture:

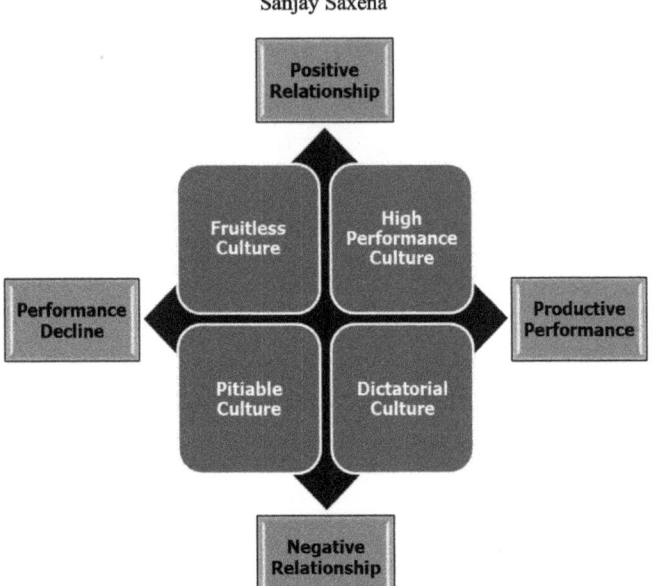

Figure 5.8: High-Performance Culture

- **Fruitless Culture**

  The warm and ineffective culture is characterized by the positive relationship between managers and subordinates but declining performance trends in the organization. The goals are agreed upon mutually, but no real measures are taken to achieve the same. The employees possess no accountability towards goal achievement. There exists communication among people, but it is sporadic and ineffective. Time is wasted on useless talks. To make subordinates happy, managers are always talking nicely and telling the only good news. The people are more involved in lip-service participation, which means lots of talks and little action. Poor performances are not confronted. There are lots of excuses for poor service and quality. Effectiveness in achieving goals and service levels is not measured. Ineffective departments are not challenged. People are complacent and nice to one another. They avoid conflicts. People all appear busy but achieve little. They are more involved in measuring the activities, not the result.

- **Pitiable Culture**

    This type of culture demonstrates negative relationships between managers and subordinates, and there are declining organizational performance trends. The boss demands performance without communicating clear goals. They maintain secrecy in the organization and do not trust people with information. Communication among employees, and between managers and subordinates is restrictive. Due to this reason, many rumors prevail in the environment. Subordinates are not allowed to participate in the decision-making process. The managers are coercive with people. The workforce is seen as lazy. People hide poor quality, mistakes, or wastage, and sometimes do not care about achieving standards. Departments do not cooperate and blame one another for poor performance. Criticism occurs behind people's backs – real fear to speak openly. There is a lot of focus on catching people doing things wrong.

- **Dictatorial Culture**

    In this type of culture, there are negative relationships between managers and subordinates, but despite negative relationships, organizational performance is positive. This is due to fear created by the management. The boss sets goals without consultation with employees. There is one-way communication that is mainly downward communication. Managers allow their subordinates to participate in decision-making according to their own needs. Managers are managing through their status and position. There are very few learning opportunities for subordinates. In this culture, there exists restrictive job boundaries and training for employees. Employees work with a mindset that the boss knows better. Quality inspectors check on conformance to standards. Quality is the managers' responsibility. People do not challenge the views or ideas of their bosses and fear challenging their managers. Management sets strict rules and checks on people all the time.

- **High-Performance Culture**

    In a high-performance organizational culture, there exists a positive relationship among the people of the organization. This relationship goes much beyond working relationships reaching into the hearts of people and generating mutual commitment for each other. Because of this intense commitment, people start caring for each other, become compassionate, and are willing to take on each other's responsibility. Also, they feel accountable for each other's successes and failures. All the employees are strongly aligned and emotionally committed to the organization's vision, mission, goals, and values. The organizational performance is positive and growing at the required pace. There is effective participation of employees in the decision-making process, and goals are determined mutually. Effective measures are mutually developed to achieve the goals. Effective two-way communication prevails in the system. There exists a democratic and open climate in the organization, and transparency is maintained in the system. People are empowered to make decisions and frame their short-term goals. There are self-directed teams that monitor and continually improve their performance.

    Everyone can contribute and is an expert in his/her own right. Quality and service are the responsibility of the person doing the job. Supply-chain integration and customer-focused goals prevail across all functions. Ideas are shared freely. People feel free to disagree with their superiors without having the fear of being victimized. All are concerned with results and outputs. People are innovative in how they do their work to achieve agreed goals. The high-performance organizational culture is adaptive, where managers pay close attention to all the organization's stakeholders and develop a partnership with them. Leadership at all levels is valued; people are encouraged to provide leadership and initiate change whenever needed to satisfy the legitimate interests of stakeholders.

Chapter 6

Measuring Outcomes

6.1 Measuring Firm's Performance

A firm's strategic performance should be evaluated to understand that firm's strategic objectives are achieved. Measuring a firm's performance is important because investors' decision to invest in the enterprise is based on the firm's performance results. Performance evaluation is not only restricted to financial outcomes, but it also comes in many forms, such as several defects, employee satisfaction, the development of IT-enabled systems, etc. To evaluate all forms of outcomes, we need metrics containing various Key Performance Indicators (KPIs), strategic targets related to selected KPIs, and strategic actions taken to achieve targets. The author has developed a Comprehensive Performance Scorecard (CPS), which is shown in figure 6.1.

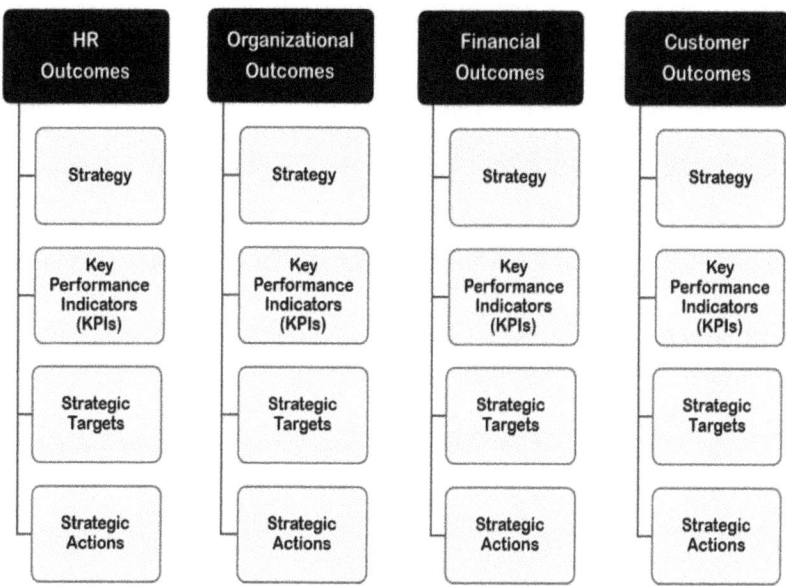

Figure 6.1: Comprehensive Performance Scorecard

The Comprehensive Performance Scorecard is a holistic management strategy by connecting chosen business strategy, KPIs, strategic targets, and strategic actions. There are four categories of outcomes included in the comprehensive performance scorecard: HR, Organizational, Financial, and Customer Outcomes. All four categories are interconnected to each other and contribute effectively to each other's outcomes. Poor outcomes in one category adversely affect the outcomes of other categories. For example, if the HR outcomes are not satisfactory, the organization cannot sustain its financial performance for a long time. Therefore, an organization must perform equally well in all categories. Equal focus and weightage should be given to each category to sustain its business in a highly competitive and turbulent environment.

The KPIs are selected based on chosen business strategy by the firm, such as low-cost strategy, differentiation strategy, blue ocean strategy, etc. Its strategic target and strategic action then follow each KPI. Selecting too many KPIs in one category of outcomes will dilute the firm's efforts; therefore, just two or three KPIs should be selected in each category to put focused efforts and generate excellent outcomes in each category.

6.2 HR Outcomes

HR OUTCOMES			
Business Strategy	**KPIs**	**Strategic Targets**	**Strategic Actions**
Low-Cost Differentiation Strategy	Citizenship Behavior	10% improvement in Citizenship Behavior Index	Enhance Employee Empowerment and Create a Sense of Ownership
	Employee Turnover	20 % Reduction in Employee Turnover	Improving Job Design, and leadership quality, enhancing Job Security, and reducing work overload.
	Employee Absenteeism	20% Reduction in Absenteeism	Improving Work-Life Balance
	Employee Satisfaction	10% improvement in Employee Satisfaction Index	Building Motivational Climate by using Two Factors Motivational Theory

Table 6.1: KPIs of HR Outcomes

HR outcomes majorly tend to satisfy employees' interests such as employees job satisfaction, work-life balance, job security, well-being, personal and professional growth, etc. In addition, the satisfaction of employees' interests leads to the achievement of various HR KPIs such as reduction in employee turnover, reduction in absenteeism, and development of citizenship behavior. Table 6.1 contains various KPIs related to HR outcomes and linked to the firm's business strategy, strategic targets, and actions.

- **Citizenship Behavior**
  Citizenship behavior describes employees' actions that go the extra mile beyond their job description. They work much more than their co-workers. They work diligently to discover innovative ways of doing things better. They invest their time to make extra efforts to portray a good image of their firm in customers' eyes. Citizenship behavior can be developed through various ways such as empowering the employees to make their decisions, inculcating a sense of ownership of the firm in them so that they should work as an owner of the firm, and providing them the freedom to fail.

- **Employee Turnover**
  Employee turnover refers to the number of employees who leave an organization and are replaced by new employees. It increases due to various reasons such as lack of growth, poor leadership qualities and coercive behavior of line managers, absence of recognition and rewards, poor job security, work overload, etc. In addition, high employee turnover increases the cost of hiring, training, and induction. As a result, line managers need to put extra time and redundant efforts into aligning new employees with the organizational vision, mission, values, practices, business strategy, and objectives.

- **Employee Absenteeism**
  Employee absenteeism occurs when employees take casual leave without any valid reason, take sick leave without being sick, or go for leave without pay. Employee absenteeism increases due to burnout, work stress, work overload, poor leadership, or low morale. Absenteeism leads to a reduction in personal as well as team productivity, which then reduces the firm's profitability and increases overall costs. Employee absenteeism can be mitigated by nurturing leadership, optimizing work overload, and improving work-life balance.
- **Employees' Satisfaction**
  It is a degree to which the employees are satisfied with their jobs. Dissatisfied employees lack motivation, possess a negative attitude, perform poorly, and destroy the team's performance. As a result, they adversely impact the bottom-line performance of the firm. For improving employee motivation, a firm must develop a motivation climate to ensure both hygiene and growth factors are in place.

6.3 Organizational Outcomes

ORGANIZATIONAL OUTCOMES			
Strategy	**KPIs**	**Strategic Targets**	**Strategic Actions**
Low-Cost Differentiation Strategy	Process Innovation	10% Improvement in Process Efficiency Index.	Reengineering the purchasing process Store management Job shop management
	Product Innovation	Two new or improved products are to be launched in the market.	10% increase in R & D investments
	Cost Reduction	10 % reduction in overall cost	Through Process Innovation and Restructuring of Organizational Structure
	Zero Defect	10% reduction in the number of defective products	Implementation of Total Quality Management

Table 6.2: KPIs of Organizational Outcomes

Today's highly competitive environment forces companies to keep improving their existing products and processes to penetrate existing markets further and satisfy their customers. Therefore, a firm needs to develop its abilities to increase cost efficiency, launch new products, develop new features in the existing products, ensure zero defects in production and improve overall productivity. Therefore, to achieve a low-cost differentiation strategy, a firm should focus mainly on KPIs such as product innovation, process innovation, zero defects, and cost reduction. Table 6.2 shows various KPIs, strategic Targets, and Strategic Actions related to organizational outcomes.

- **Process Innovation**
  Process innovation is a new or improved way of doing things to increase production scales, reduce the cost of operations, and eliminate the number of defects in production. Process innovation may include reengineering the linkage and flow of various activities and utilizing new equipment, technology, and software.

- **Product Innovation**
  Product innovation is the development of new products, but this also includes redesigning the existing products into better products regarding improvements in quality and overall performance, adding new features, and using new raw materials for manufacturing the existing product.

6.4 Financial Outcomes

FINANCIAL OUTCOMES			
Strategy	**KPIs**	**Strategic Targets**	**Strategic Actions**
Low-Cost Differentiation Strategy	Sales Revenue	30% growth over last year's sales revenue	New Product Launch Strengthening the dealer network Focus on institutional sales
	Profit	20% growth over last year's profit	By increasing sales revenue and reducing the cost

	Stock Value	20% increase in stock price	By increasing the sales revenue, profits, and Internal Rate of Return
	Market Share	5% growth over last year's market share	By increasing the number of dealers and institutional accounts

Table 6.3: KPIs of Financial Outcomes

The financial outcomes of a firm contribute to its financial health of a firm. Table 6.3 is showing various KPIs and their Strategic Targets and Strategic Actions to achieve the firm's low-cost differentiation strategy. These KPIs are the firm's sales revenue, profits, stock value, and market share.

- **Sales revenue**

  In accounting, the term 'sales or 'revenue' are used interchangeably, which means both are the same. Sales or revenue is the income received by a company from its sales of goods or the provision of services. Sales revenue is not always in cash form; it can be cash receivable because of sales made on credit.

- **Profits**

  Profit describes the financial benefit realized when the revenue generated from a business activity exceeds the expenses, costs, and taxes involved in sustaining the activity in question. Any profit earned siphons back to business owners, who choose to either reinvest the cash back into the business or utilize it as an investment in other businesses. Profit is calculated as Total Revenue – Total Expenses.

- **Stock Value**

  A stock (also known as equity) is a security that represents the ownership of a portion of a corporation. This entitles the stock owner to a proportion of the corporation's assets and profits equal to how much stock they own. Units of stock are called "shares." The value of a stock is a corporation's ability to create a return, to create income, or again in value for the investor.

- **Market Share**

  Out of the total sales of products generated in a market, the percentage goes to a company that defines its market share. In other words, if a total of 1000 units of products are sold and 100 of which are from one company, that company holds (100/1000 x 100) 10% market share.

6.5 Customer Outcomes

CUSTOMER OUTCOMES			
Strategy	**KPIs**	**Strategic Targets**	**Strategic Actions**
Low-Cost Differentiation Strategy	Customer Retention	10% growth over existing retained Customers	Providing exceptional buying experience, extra mile services after sales, Reducing post-purchase dissonance
	Customer Addition	10% growth over an existing number of dealers and	Tapping new dealers and new institutional accounts

		institutional accounts	
	Customer Satisfaction	10% Improvement in Customers' Satisfaction Index	New, improved quality products, affordable price, amazing buying experience, exceptional after-sales service

Table 6.4: KPIs of Customer Outcomes

Customer outcomes satisfy the customers' interests. Customers want products or services that can satisfy their needs and wants at affordable prices. All firms want to provide maximum value to their customers in the form of products and services. Customers' main concerns are the quality, performance, and price of the products they buy and use. A firm can retain existing customers and add new customers only when their concerns are satisfied. Therefore, as shown in Table 6.4., the KPIs related to customer outcomes are customer retention, customer addition, and customer satisfaction.

- **Customer Retention**

According to Harvard Business School's study, increasing customer retention rates by 5 percent increases profits by 25 to 95 percent. Experts in sales and marketing know that it costs four to five times more to get a new customer than to keep an existing one.

- **Customers Addition**
  Acquiring new customers is important if a firm wants steady growth in the market. On average, a company loses 15 – 20 percent of its customers every year, therefore, a firm needs to acquire new customers every year to replenish the drain generated by customers' attrition. Some of the common causes of customer attrition are customer dissatisfaction, customer business failure, deep economic recession, or the death of a customer.

- **Customers Satisfaction**
  Customer satisfaction can be defined as measuring how products and services from the company meet or exceed customers' expectations and how happy they are. The customer's happiness index helps business owners to improve their products and services.

References

1. Ansoff, H. Igor, (1957). "Strategies for diversification". Harvard Business Review, Vol. 35 Issue 5, pp. 113-124.
2. Barney, J. B., & Hesterly, W. S., (2010). VRIO Framework. In Strategic Management and Competitive Advantage (pp. 68–86). New Jersey: Pearson.
3. Barney, J.B., (1991). Firm Resources and Sustained Competitive Advantage. Journal of Management, Vol. 17.
4. Barney, J.B., (1995). Looking Inside for Competitive Advantage. Academy of Management Executive, Vol.9. Issue 4,
5. Barney, Jay, "Firm Resources and Sustained Competitive Advantage". Journal of Management. 17 (1): 99–120. (1 March 1991).
6. Christensen, p, (1997). xviii. Christensen describes as "revolutionary" innovations as "discontinuous" "sustaining innovations."
7. Christensen, Clayton M.; Dillon, Karen; Hall, Taddy; Duncan, David, (2016). "Know your customer's Job To Be Done", Harvard Business Review.
8. Christensen, Clayton M.; Dillon, Karen; Hall, Taddy; Duncan, David, (2016). Competing Against Luck, New York, New York, USA: HarperBusiness, ISBN 978-0062435613. The Story of Innovation and Customer Choice.
9. Clayton M. Christensen, Taddy Hall, Karen Dillon, David S. Duncan. Competing Against Luck: The Story of Innovation and Customer Choice. Harper Collins.
10. Clayton M. Christensen, (1997). The Innovator's Dilemma. When New Technologies Cause Great Firms to Fail. Harvard Business Review Press.
11. Csikszentmihályi M, (1990). FLOW: The Psychology of Optimal Experience (PDF). Harper and Row. ISBN 978-0-06-016253-5.
12. Edmund P. Learned, C. Roland Christiansen, Kenneth Andrews, and William D. Guth, (1969). Business Policy, Text, and Cases. Homewood, IL: Irwin.

13. G. Johnson, R. Whittington, and K. Scholes, (2012). "Fundamentals of Strategy," Pearson Education.
14. Henderson Bruce, Henderson, (1979). Corporate Strategy, Harper Collins.
15. Henderson, Bruce. "The Product Portfolio". Retrieved 3 April 2013.
16. Herzberg, Frederick, (1966). Work and the Nature of Man. Cleveland: World Publishing. OCLC 243610.
17. Herzberg, Frederick, (January–February 1964). "The Motivation-Hygiene Concept and Problems of Manpower". Personnel Administration (27): 3–7.
18. Herzberg, Frederick, Mausner, Bernard; Snyderman, Barbara B., (1959). The Motivation to Work (2nd ed.). New York: John Wiley. ISBN 0471373893.
19. J., Aguilar, F. (1967). Scanning the business environment. Macmillan. OCLC 495475137.
20. Katzenbach et al., (2003). The Wisdom of Teams, Harper Business.
21. Kim, W. C.; Mauborgne, R., (2004). Blue Ocean Strategy: How to Create Uncontested Market Space and Make the Competition Irrelevant. Boston: Harvard Business School Press. ISBN 978-1591396192.
22. Kim, W. Chan; Mauborgne, Renée (2004). "Blue Ocean Strategy: From Theory to Practice". California Management Review. 47 (3): 105–121.
23. Kotter, John P. (1995-05-01). "Leading Change: Why Transformation Efforts Fail". Harvard Business Review. ISSN 0017-8012
24. Maslow, Abraham H. (1943). "A theory of human motivation". Psychological Review. 50 (4): 370–396.
25. Porter M.E., (2008). The Five Competitive Forces That Shape Strategy. Harvard Business Review,
26. Porter, M.E., (Nov/Dec 1996). "What is Strategy," Harvard Business Review.
27. Porter, Michael E. (1980). Competitive Strategy. Free Press. ISBN 0-684-84148-7.

28. Porter, Michael E. (1985). Competitive Advantage. Free Press. ISBN 0-684-84146-0.
29. Porter, Michael E. (1985). Competitive Advantage: Creating and Sustaining Superior Performance. New York.: Simon and Schuster. ISBN 9781416595847.
30. Porter. M.E., (1985). Competitive Advantage: Creating and Sustaining Superior Performance. The Free Press.
31. Schein, Edgar H. (1990). "Organizational culture". American Psychologist. 45 (2): 109–119. doi:10.1037/0003-066X.45.2.109.
32. Silva, Carlos Nunes (2005). "SWOT analysis". In Caves, Roger W. (ed.). Encyclopedia of the city. Abingdon; New York: Routledge. pp. 444–445. doi:10.4324/9780203484234. ISBN 978-0415862875. OCLC 55948158.
33. Thompson J. and Martin F., (2010). Strategic Management: Awareness & Change. 6th ed. Cengage Learning EMEA.
34. Walshe, K./ Harvey, G./ Hyde, P./ Pandit, N. (2004): Organizational Failure and Turnaround: Lessons for Public Services from the For-Profit Sector, in Public Money & Management, Vol. 24, No. 4 (August, 2004), pp. 201–208. (p. 204).

www.ingramcontent.com/pod-product-compliance
Lightning Source LLC
LaVergne TN
LVHW061544070526
838199LV00077B/6896